Rechtsvergleichung und Rechtsvereinheitlichung

herausgegeben von der

Gesellschaft für Rechtsvergleichung e.V.

106

Southern Lessons for Constitutional Law

Proceedings of the 39th Congress of the Society of Comparative Law in Berlin, September 12 to 14, 2024

Edited by

Uwe Kischel

Mohr Siebeck

Uwe Kischel is professor of public law, European law and comparative law at the University of Greifswald.

ISBN 978-3-16-170598-4 / eISBN 978-3-16-170599-1
DOI 10.1628/978-3-16-170599-1

ISSN 1861-5449 / eISSN 2569-426X (Rechtsvergleichung und Rechtsvereinheitlichung)

The Deutsche Nationalbibliothek lists this publication in the Deutsche Nationalbibliographie; detailed bibliographic data are available at *https://dnb.dnb.de.*

Printed on non-aging paper.

Mohr Siebeck GmbH & Co. KG, Wilhelmstraße 18, 72074 Tübingen, Germany
www.mohrsiebeck.com, info@mohrsiebeck.com

Preface

The general topic of the 39th congress of the Society of Comparative Law "Global North – Global South" has until now received scant attention in German constitutional law and in other European constitutional systems. Against this backdrop, the session of the Section of Comparative Public Law tried to identify the specific *legal* implications of this topic by examining the practical influence of perspectives from the Global South on constitutional law.

Traditional comparative constitutional scholarship has focused primarily on legal ideas, concepts and institutions originating in countries such as the United States, England, Germany, France – i.e. in the Global North –, analyzing, for example, how these legal elements function and how they might be modified in different Northern, but also Southern jurisdictions. To increase the focus on the Global South, this perspective needs to be shifted and supplemented by asking which contributions the Global South made to the international discussion on constitutional law, and by viewing these contributions not only from a Northern, but also from a Southern point of view.

The Section of Comparative Public Law addressed this question of "Southern Lessons for Constitutional Law", in a first part, by examining specific regional and country perspectives as well as the way they interact in the sense of "regards croisés". A second part then explored, in the form of case studies, concrete legal fields in which direct contributions by the Global South to the international discourse on constitutional law seemed particularly evident.

This volume compiles all public law contributions to the 39th Congress, and reflects the dual structure of the session itself. In a first group, the authors take regards croisés on the question of Southern lessons for constitutional law: Philipp Dann with a view from Germany, Konrad Lachmayer with a view from Austria, Pablo Riberi with a view from South America, and Surya Deva with a view from Asia. The second group contains two case studies of Southern influences: Selin Esen explores implications for the rule of law, while David Bilchitz examines socio-economic rights across the North-South divide. Collectively, these papers critically engage the transformative potential of Southern constitutional thought.

As editor of this volume, I would like to express my sincere gratitude to the authors for their remarkable contributions, and for the timely submission of their manuscripts. I particularly thank the Secretary of the Section of Comparative Public Law, Prof. Dr. Sebastian Graf von Kielmansegg, for his indispensable support in organizing the session. His calm and constant work in the background made our session the smooth experience that it was. I would also like to thank my assistants Carla Blecke, Christine Hecker, Clemens Sonntag, and William Kopplow, as well as my students Luca Boddenberg, Lea Freitag, Michaela Hentze, Moritz Kellotat, Josephin Lange, Jens Noske, Konstantin Oppeneiger, Liam Piwodda, Lara Rathsack, and Tim Sack for their invaluable assistance.

Greifswald, June 2025 Uwe Kischel

Table of Contents

Southern Lessons for Constitutional Law – A view from Germany

Philipp Dann

The topic of 'Learning from the Global South' constitutes a very timely choice for this conference of the German Society of Comparative Law. In my understanding, it represents one of the three major challenges of our age – alongside digitalization and climate change – that cut across many fields and therefore not merely can, but should be adopted from various disciplinary perspectives and positionalities.

Against this backdrop, the structure of my presentation reflects on four central questions: the first two questions examine preliminary considerations, yet they are followed by two questions that go to the heart of the conference's subject as articulated by the organisers. First, I will inquire the implication of the 'Global South' and the possible meaning of this notion. Second, I will consider whether it is appropriate to resort to the standard toolbox of comparative law to analyse constitutional law in the Global South or whether there is something distinct about this law. I will then turn to the main questions as posed by the organisers: What are the constitutional experiences of the Global South and hence the lessons we can draw from those experiences? Finally, I will reflect on the distinct perspective from Germany: What does it mean to engage with this discourse from a German standpoint? Which contributions can German scholars as well as German law make to this discussion?

A. What is the Global South?

This presentation commences with a crucial question: What is the Global South? There are, of course, many positions and inputs on this certainly difficult and contested notion.[1] It is important to appreciate, first and foremost, that the notion is a designation that is not regional. It does not refer exclusively to Africa, Asia, or Latin America, but cuts across and transcends those regional categories. Likewise, it is also not an ideological designation. It does not denote, for instance,

[1] *Philipp Dann*, Southern Turn, Northern implications, Comparative Constitutional Studies 1 (2023), p. 57; *Siba Grogovui*, A Revolution Nevertheless, The Global South, Vol. 5 (2011), p. 175.

socialist or *liberal* constitutionalism. So apparently, the notion does cut into something else than a regional or an ideological category.

To some extent, it is perhaps easier to grasp what it does *not* mean; what is *not* the Global South. It is not a geographic description; that much is already clear by the adjective *global*. Some countries typically considered as North or 'First World' are located in the Southern hemisphere, such as Australia; at the same time, the Global South can also be found in Europe – if not even within Germany. Moreover, the term should not be conflated with the 'Third World', the originally very proudly used but since the 1980s increasingly deranged and hierarchical notion that was popular up until the 1990s.[2] It is also not the designation or the label that is mostly used in the United Nations, where it is 'developing countries' and neither is it synonymous with 'low-income countries' as categorized by the World Bank.[3]

The Global South then, admittedly, is a somewhat difficult and elusive concept. But being a German lawyer, I am inclined to provide a 'working definition' in order to better grasp and delimitate the core of present discussions. I propose that the label Global South designates those countries and societies that are part of a periphery created by European colonialism and that remain in this periphery due to the continuing legacies and effects of said colonialism.

My central argument and defining aspect then is that we can only understand and use the notion of Global South once we begin to understand, or at least try to understand the nature of European colonialism – what it constituted and how it continues to produce effects in the present. The notion of the Global South is one that is deeply informed by history, informed by political economy and one that signals a certain sensibility for understanding the margins, for understanding the centre and periphery relation.[4] Thus, while the Global South cannot be reduced to a mere geographic notion, it is also not simply an economic concept. Rather it has a much broader, more politically charged meaning.

Nonetheless, it is a notion that has been criticised and in the context of said criticism I would like to engage with three frequently raised objections: One is that the term is simplifying exceedingly. How can one neatly divide the world into merely two spheres? Hence, critics suggest these labels of 'South' and 'North' expressing an unreasonable broad concept. Latin America, China, and India are diverse to a point where they seem like different worlds, so how can one put them together? It is my contention, that this critique fails to get to the core of the

[2] *Ulrich Menzel*, Das Ende der Dritten Welt und das Scheitern der großen Theorien, 1992; *Vijay Prashad*, The Darker Nations: A People's History of the Third World, 2007, p. 6; *Sundhya Pahuja*, Decolonizing International Law, 2014, p. 9.

[3] *Philipp Dann*, The Law of Development Cooperation, 2013, p. 202.

[4] *Jean Comaroff*, John Comaroff, Theory from the South, or How Euro-America is evolving towards Africa, 2011; *Florian Hoffmann*, Facing South: On the Significance of An/Other Modernity in Comparative Constitutional Law, in: Philipp Dann, Michael Riegner, Maxim Bönnemann (eds.), The Global South and Comparative Constitutional Law, 2020, p. 41.

notion. The main idea behind using the notion of the Global South is rather to reassert the ongoing relevance of the centre-periphery divide. And all of these regions share the common experience of having been profoundly shaped by colonialism – albeit in surely very different and multifaceted ways.

The second major criticism is that the notion itself might ultimately be reifying problematic categories; that by using South and North again we just continue to solidify a distinction between two halves of the world, which we actually aspire to overcome. This is an undeniably valid and thoughtful argument addressing a serious problem. Yet again, such concerns, while they rightfully are important, should not lead to abandoning the concept altogether. The world, after all, is not a level playing field. The recognition of existing distinctions, which we must have to learn with, is thus of fundamental importance. These distinctions should be openly addressed rather than to obscure them.

The final point of criticism is that the term 'Global South' is, in fact, a notion of the North about the South. As was pointed out frequently, it is not a notion that is very popular in the South, for example in India or in Latin America. Tellingly, a Chilean student of mine remarked never having used the notion of the Global South in Chile or in other Latin American countries. So interestingly, it is a label that enjoys popularity in Europe and in North America, but appears to be mostly absent in the contexts it seeks to designate.

In conclusion, even this paradoxical observation might complement the overall picture: Global South remains a complicated notion raising a lot of questions, it nonetheless carries weight and fulfils an important function as it points to distinctions that continue to have relevance. Ultimately, it displays the gap of which side we as societies stood during the colonial period visible. Were we in the centre? Were we colonizers? Or were we the colonized? Those questions continue to have an effect on and to shape our present realities. The notion of the Global South helps us to see that. In conclusion, it may be imperfect, albeit valuable and even necessary to point to an important fault line, to a distinction that continues to be relevant.

B. Can we use the normal toolbox of comparative law?

Once a common understanding of the notion of the Global South is established and once one decides to work with it, the question remains how to proceed. What kind of methodology should be applied? Is it suitable to have recourse to the standard toolbox of comparative law? Is it sufficient to be aware of the concepts of functionalism, protectionism, critical comparison; that there are all these kinds of different approaches to be able to start working on 'Southern Lessons from Constitutional Law'?[5]

[5] For good overviews, see *Uwe Kischel*, Comparative Law, 2019; *Mathias Siems*, Comparative Law, 2022.

This question should be strongly disagreed with. On the contrast, one should not simply proceed with the existing methodology. I would argue that its approaches cannot be applied unconditionally unless and until we have started to consider the legacies of colonialism also in this regard. Moreover, I do believe that until this point, our comparative law methodologies, our understandings and critiques of functionalism and contextualism etc., do not take this dimension enough into account. This displays a significant problem and if we want to have a serious engagement, we need to fill this gap. I am sceptical of those who just add India, Columbia, or Tanzania to the gene pool of comparative (law) studies without taking into account the larger, more complex and more painful history. It is unlikely that progress will be achieved if we restrain from finally addressing this.[6]

Accordingly, what does this demand mean concretely for constitutional scholarship? How can we reflect the legacies of colonialism when we analyse constitutional orders? In this second section, I will raise three problems indicating what needs to be infused in our methodological thinking as we proceed. These are well-known problems to some extent, but I still consider it important to make them transparent.

The first one is an epistemic problem that concerns the asymmetry of knowledge recognition. It touches upon classic questions of who is heard and what we actually think to know. Daniel Bonilla Maldonado, a famous comparative law scholar from Colombia[7], once shared a telling story about his two email addresses with me. One email address is his usual Colombian email address. He works in Los Andes, which is one of the great universities in Latin America – but then he also studied and worked at Yale. Correspondingly, he had an email address from Yale as well. With these two addresses, he had a very disparate experience: When he used the Yale address, he got immediate responses, usually within a day. When he used the Colombian address, he did not receive an immediate answer – if he received one at all. This example illustrates a crucial epistemic point: It does make a considerable difference where people think you are from. It is perhaps not the name, but the origin. A Colombian origin may or may not arouse interest. However, being affiliated with Yale will most likely do: Yale is perceived as important. This leads to a rephrased version of Gayatri Spivak's pertinent question 'Can the Subaltern speak'?[8] Is there actually anything relevant to learn from the Subaltern, i.e., in our context the South? Do we as scholars from the Global North even want to listen and to consider Southern knowledge as relevant? By posing these ques-

[6] *Ran Hirschl*, Comparative Matters: The Renaissance of Comparative Constitutional Law, 2014, p. 218.

[7] *Daniel Bonilla Maldonado*, Constitutionalism of the Global South, 2014; *Daniel Bonilla Maldonado*, Legal Barbarians: Identity, Modern Cómparative Law and the Global South, 2022.

[8] *Gayatri Spivak*, Can the Subaltern Speak?, reprint 2010; *Gayatri Spivak*, Critique of Postcolonial Reason, 1999.

tions, we come to realize the extent to which we lack immediate direct knowledge, voices, and positions from the Global South. In our literature we still have an immense imbalance of recognized voices. We must commence by at least acknowledging this and investing more efforts in making us hear and comprehend voices and positions from the Global South. Simultaneously, we will not solve the problem by entering a library in order to about Southern jurisdictions. That is epistemically not sufficient. Instead, it is fundamental to put much more effort into direct and open-minded exchanges. Only then can it is possible to address this first problem and better understand what we actually do (not) know and start recognizing the asymmetries in the scholarly recognition of produced knowledge.

The second problem is one that touches upon the core of the factual working conditions in the Global South and is to some extent profane. However, the institutional problems underlying knowledge production must also be acknowledged. We must come to realize how difficult it is to produce books and writing and the like in the material circumstances described as the Global South.[9] To illustrate this point with yet another personal observation: Many universities in India are not like this conference building here at Humboldt University. They are not palaces; they do not have massive libraries and other such facilities. Instead, they are often highly instable institutions that are equally often exposed to political pressure, where teaching and grading obligations of colleagues are suffocating. Often, professors work in part time jobs, they do not certainly have the time and leisure to read, to write, to engage, or to rethink. While I am taking most of my insight from personal experiences with India, these conditions are probably comparable to many places in the Global South. The Indian law schools are just a different kind of world when we compare them with German universities. To be clear, I am neither talking about intelligence nor commitments of the scholars. Rather, I am talking about the institutional context, in which people can produce knowledge, can write, and find the time to reflect on writing. All this needs to be taken into account, next to the partly challenging circumstances of life in many parts of the Global South. We as scholars must seek ways to acknowledge that, even though it does not fit neatly into a methodological category. But it is a sensibility that we have to bring to the topic and that we have to bring to the conversation if we aspire to engage with scholarship and scholars of the Global South.

My third and last point is more theoretical and also more established. I think we should increase our awareness for the deceitful universality of our constitutional vocabulary. In our constitutional as well as our political theory, we assume that we all share the same vocabulary. When talking about states, rights, borders, about representative democracy, or similar concepts, we assume that we all mean

---

[9] *Dinesha Samararatne*, Comparative Constitutional Law from and within the Global South: challenges, prospects and hope, World Comparative Law (VRÜ-WCL) 57 (2024), p. 337.

the same thing. But this assumption alone is highly deceptive.[10] In my view, it is even a mistake, because these notions necessarily rest on local experiences and stories that are profoundly diverse. We need to understand and somehow integrate those crucial differences into a more differentiated and reflective vocabulary. This adds to the existing critiques that problematize functionalist approaches, because it once more lays bare the difficulty to even agree on the use of any kind of common vocabulary.

In summary, the illustrated three problems cause methodological challenges that we must factor in when looking for lessons from the Global South. I do not view these challenges as insurmountable; rather, we might eventually be able to overcome them if we accept to work on them. What I deem essential though, is that we approach these difficulties with intellectual honesty and rigour to find out how to overcome them together.

C. What are distinct Southern constitutional experiences – and hence lessons for law?

To move on and beyond these more preliminary considerations, I now come to the main question and that is first of all: what are the distinct Southern lessons? Allow me to amend this question a little by pointing out that any lessons follow from certain distinct experiences. Asking about constitutional experiences made in the South is, of course, a slightly broader topic but it builds the groundwork from which then concrete lessons follow. Let me therefore note three distinct Southern experiences of which special emphasis will rest on the third.[11]

The first are experiences that originate in the social and economic legacies of colonialism. Many countries that we consider part of the Global South are still in the periphery of global capitalism. There is widespread and deep poverty and we need to be aware of those imbalances and inequalities. Not least, because they also have an effect on constitutionalism, namely that the material promise of constitutionalism is much stronger in Southern constitutions.[12] Against this

[10] On this point famously *Dipesh Chakrabarty*, Provincializing Europe, 2004; *Upendra Baxi*, Constitutionalism as a Site of State Formative Practice, Cardozo Law Review 21 (2000), p. 1183; *Daniel Bonilla Maldonado*, Constitutionalism in the Global South, 2014, p. 18, Introduction.

[11] In more detail: *Philipp Dann*, Michael Riegner, Maxim Bönnemann, The Southern Turn in Comparative Constitutional Law: An Introduction, in: Ibid (eds.), The Global South and Comparative Constitutional Law, 2020, p. 23.

[12] *David Bilchitz*, Socio-Economic Rights and Expanding Access to Justice in South Africa: What can be done?, in: Philipp Dann, Michael Riegner, Maxim Bönnemann (eds.), The Global South and Comparative Constitutional Law, 2020, p. 210; *Roberto Gagarella*, Inequality and the Constitution, in: Philipp Dann, Michael Riegner, Maxim Bönnemann (eds.), The Global South and Comparative Constitutional Law, 2020, p. 235.

backdrop, it is certainly no coincidence that the notion of transformative constitutionalism emerged in South Africa and was soon picked up in India and in Latin America. It carries a certain kind of hope but also a certain urgency to react and to call upon the state to deal with social economic legacies.[13] That is one area of distinctly Southern experiences.

The other constitutional experience that emerges connects to the political legacies of colonialism. We cannot forget about those either. It starts with the emergence and genesis of statehood in Europe versus what we call the South.[14] European states emerged over centuries of competition in Europe, over centuries of competition between sacral and profane power. This was a very slow process of building up state capacities, of negotiating borders and after many centuries, as late as in the 19th century, it somehow gelled into what we know today as a state. The story in the South is, of course, decisively different and this mostly has to do with European intrusion, interference and colonialism. Boarders in the Global South are very often contingent and contingently drawn up by colonial powers. There was almost no time to build up state capacities – existing capacities were even destroyed. The consequences of this history are seen in many political constellations in the South today, in deeply divided societies and in contested borders. The question of how a state's constitution emerged under these circumstances and how it operates in these contexts points to an entirely different kind of inquiry than for their European counterparts.

This leads directly to the third point which is the contestation of constitutionalism. Once again, I begin in Germany and perhaps from what German scholars assume to be the normal case. In my opinion we should be well aware of the German – conscious or sub-conscious and somewhat Hegelian – assumption that the state is pursuing the common good.[15] I think this assumption is deeply engraved in almost all German lawyers. We just assume that the state overall is a somewhat benevolent and neutral force. Of course, there are different parties competing for power, but ultimately the state is good, with political pluralism perhaps even serving as a reason to prove that point. So, that reflects a foundational German understanding. We have a certain trust in that framework.

---

[13] *Frans Viljoen, Oscar Vilhena, Upendra Baxi* (eds.), Transformative constitutionalism: Comparing the apex courts of Brazil, India and South Africa, 2013; *Gautam Bhatia*, Transformative Constitution. A Radical Biography in Nine Acts, HarperCollins India, 2019; *Armin von Bogdandy, Eduardo Ferrer Mac-Gregor, Mariela Morales Antoniazzi, Flávia Piovesan, Ximena Soley* (eds.), Transformative constitutionalism in Latin America. The emergence of a new Ius Commune, 2017; *Philipp Dann*, Transformative Constitutionalism and the Indian Constitution, in: Aparna Chandra, Gautam Bhatia, Niraya Gopal (eds.), Cambridge Companion to the Indian Constitution, 2025 (forthcoming).

[14] For a very elegant version of this argument through the lens of Max Weber's influence on our vocabulary, see *Florian Hoffmann*, Facing South, in: Philipp Dann, Michael Riegner, Maxim Bönnemann (eds.), The Global South and Comparative Constitutional Law, 2020, p. 41.

[15] *Michael Stolleis*, Geschichte des Öffentlichen Rechts, Vol. 2 (2017), p. 133.

But this is miles apart from the assumption about statehood and about constitutionalism in many countries, in many societies of the Global South. Frequently, the state there is not perceived as that neutral, common good pursuing kind of creature, but, on the contrary, as partisan, as aggressive, as overbearing, and as a problem.[16]

With the perception of the state being very different, that naturally also impacts the constitutional framework. We have that highly idealized Euro-American understanding of the founding moment, of a revolution, an assembly of the people coming together, writing the framework of the society – a well-known story.[17] But we must not assume that the same understanding of the story is correct in many countries of the Global South. Often constitution making was highly contested and is contested until today.[18] So, our falling back on a fairly trusting assumption of statehood and of the constitution as a neutral framework of a political discourse is not universal but rather particular. In extension, we need to see and understand that the expectations towards as well as the working of constitutions are different elsewhere.

To conclude this third section, it becomes evident that we have very contested legacies of modernity in constitutional law and so far, there is only little understanding of these contestations in Europe. But we must be acutely aware of these contestations when we operate in the Global South. I think it is imperative to be much more mindful and knowledgeable about the main stories of emerging nations, emerging statehoods, or emerging legal orders in the Global South before we even start to get closer to a meaningful engagement. In that sense, these are very important experiences and lessons from the South.

D. What is the view from Germany?

I finally come to the view from Germany. I will establish three ideas which follow from what has just been established. The first is a direct follow-up to the previous thought: there is a strong need to parochialize our own constitutional experience. We as Germans are often proud of our *Grundgesetz* and there are good reasons to

---

[16] *Anuj Bhuwania*, Judicial Review and India's Statist Transformative Constitutionalism, in: Aparna Chandra, Guathm Bhatia, Niraja Gopal Jayal (eds.), Cambridge Companion to the Indian Constitution, 2025 (forthcoming).

[17] *Ernst Wolfgang Böckenförde*, The Constituent Power of the People, in: Ibid., Constitutional and Political Theory, 2017; for a critical perspective from a comparative perspective *Philipp Dann, Zaid Al-Ali* (eds.), The Internationalized Pouvoir Constituant: Constitution-Making under External Influence, Max Planck United Nations Yearbook 10 (2006), p. 423.

[18] *H W O Okoth-Ogendo*, Constitutions without Constitutionalism: Reflections on an African Paradox, in: Douglas Greenberg, Stanley Katz, Melanie Beth Oliviero, Steven Wheatley (eds.), Constitutionalism and Democracy: Transitions in the Contemporary World, 1993, p. 65; *Upendra Baxi*, Constitutionalism as a Site of State Formative Practice, Cardozo Law Review 21 (2000), p. 1183.

be. But we need to realize and to be much more aware that this is our particular story, not a universal one. We cannot expect similar kinds of beliefs, trust and experiences somewhere else. Ultimately, it is crucial to understand that universality in constitutional vocabulary and in constitutional processes must be distrusted to some extent. We must make more efforts to relativise our Hegelian trust and to become more mindful of others. That is, in my view, particularly important in the German context.

The second point might almost have become obvious by now. We need to live up to our colonial history. Colonialism is also part of our history. It has been overshadowed in much of our collective memory by the Nazi era and rightfully so. I am not discounting this in any way. But I think we are catching up on studying and understanding better the colonial past of Germany, too.[19] We might currently even be ahead of similar discussions in France, in the UK, in Italy or elsewhere and generally on a good way.[20] But there is still a lot to do. Very concretely, one could now talk about restitution of artefacts, one could talk about reparations and last, but not least, in my opinion, one of the tasks of our generation is to diversify the scholarly community. So far, we are a scholarly community of constitutional law in Germany that shares a certain homogenous background and I deem it necessary and expect to see that more racialized people are integrated into that community.

Finally, we also must reflect on the blind spots that follow from that story and that composition of our scholarly community.[21] One such blind spot has become visible with respect to the German academic and public discourse on the conflict in Gaza. There is, in general, a limited awareness in Germany about the history and political complexities of the Near East. In this context, learning from the Global South also means to look at the world not from the centre but from the periphery, to study and to approach it with much more empathy or openness for the solidarity for those who have fought from the margins and not from the centre. That is somehow part of the struggles we are facing here right now. But I am an optimist. I think we are on the right path. I think we are asking these questions, but these are hard questions and we have to address them.

---

[19] *Sebastian Conrad*, German Colonialism, 2014; *Sebastian Conrad*, Rückkehr des Verdrängten? Erinnerungen an den Kolonialismus, Aus Politik und Zeitgeschichte (ApUZ) 69 (2019), p. 28.

[20] *Philipp Dann, Isabel Feichtner, Jochen von Bernstorff* (eds.), (Post)Koloniale Rechtswissenschaft, 2022; *Jakob Zollmann*, Koloniale Herrschaft und ihre Grenzen, 2010.

[21] *A Dirk Moses*, German Intellectuals and the Nazi Past, 2007.

E. Conclusion

In conclusion, I do not wish to give a mono-causal explanation for the complexities any meaningful exchange must face. In that sense, I am not arguing that colonialism is the sole explanatory factor. Rather, I think it is the other way around. We cannot get anywhere unless we also consider the colonial legacies. Especially as scholars of comparative law, we must undertake this effort as failing to do so will miss the core of the problem. Simultaneously, I do think that we are in an important and potentially very productive moment in comparative scholarship. The fact that the German Society of Comparative Law chose this topic today has meaning: we are getting better equipped to start collaborations, to learn, to engage in meaningful exchanges across the globe.

Southern Lessons for Constitutional Law – A view from Austria

Konrad Lachmayer

A. A world to discover

I. Austria's ignorance

Austria is one of the richest countries in the world[1] with (still) a good system of social security. It can be clearly understood as a social state.[2] In contrast to this, the Austrian Constitution does not contain a social state clause like in Germany[3] nor (significant) social rights[4]. This is not only reflected by case law of the Austrian Constitutional Court[5] but can also be seen in a consensus in Austrian constitutional scholarship: "To put it positively: the welfare state is not dependent on constitutional law. To put it negatively: the social constitution is almost irrelevant for the welfare state. Its value lies on another level. We are at the limit of the steering power of constitutional law."[6] The quote reflects a critical view of whether social rights can contribute to a social system at all. This perspective can be contrasted with social rights developments around the world in the last decades.[7]

---

[1] Austria ranks around top 20 with 56,506 USD GDP per capita. See https://data.worldbank.org/indicator/NY.GDP.PCAP.CD?most_recent_value_desc=true accessed 25 August 2025.

[2] *Hubert Höllmüller*, 'The Austrian Welfare State: A Halfway House' in Maja G Mitev (ed.), Social Work and Social Policy Transformations in Central and Southeast Europe (Springer Publishing 2024) 17–34.

[3] See Art. 20 para 1 German Basic Law.

[4] But see the Right to Education (Art. 2 Protocol No. 1 ECHR) or a Right of Children to Protection and Care (Art. 1 Austrian Federal Constitutional Act on the Rights of the Child).

[5] See e.g. Austrian Constitutional Court (ACC), 4.12.2023, G197/2023: "Finally, the Constitutional Court also does not share the concerns of the applicant regarding the right to the protection of property: Regulations on a pension increase generally do not interfere with this fundamental right and, according to the ECtHR's case law, Article 1 Additional Protocol No. 1 of the ECHR does not guarantee a right, social benefits or pension payments of any kind or amount as long as this is not provided for in the domestic statutory law."

[6] *Ewald Wiederin*, 'Sozialstaatlichkeit im Spannungsfeld von Eigenverantwortung und Fürsorge' in Christoph Enders and others (eds.), Der Sozialstaat in Deutschland und Europa (De Gruyter 2005) 53 (80).

[7] See below.

A deeper engagement with legal orders outside Europe, however, did not happen in the Austrian debate about social rights.[8]

If we think of Southern lessons for Austrian constitutional law, there is still a world to discover. Neither the Austrian Parliament nor the Austrian Constitutional Court regularly refer to constitutional orders outside Europe in their legal practice. While scholarship increasingly produces contributions with comparative aspects to other parts of the world, again it would usually refer to the Global North, especially to the U.S.[9] Studies in the context of the Global South are rare.[10] If they exist, however, they do not create a major impact neither on Austrian constitutional scholarship nor on Austrian constitutional practice.[11] The Austrian approach of comparative constitutional studies with regard to the Global South, thus, can be significantly improved.

II. Austria's failed colonialism and its underdeveloped development cooperation

1. Colonialism?

To understand Austria's approach towards the Global South, it seems useful to take a brief look at Austria's attitude towards colonialism in the last centuries.[12] Although Austria is a relatively small country in central Europe, it has been an empire more than 100 years ago. The Austrian Empire can serve as an example of failed colonial attempts in the 18th century, such as in Maputo Bay (Mozambique) or the Nicobar Islands (Indian Ocean).[13] While e.g. Belgian or German cruelties in Africa are well known and documented nowadays as colonialism of the 19th century,[14] the Austro-Hungarian Empire tried, but was not successful in establishing colonies, as at that time the world was already divided by (mainly) Euro-

[8] But see e.g. *Christina Binder* and others (eds.), Corporate Social Responsibility and Social Rights: Proceedings of the 5th Vienna Workshop on International Constitutional Law (Facultas Publishing/Nomos Publishing 2010).

[9] See, in this regard, for example *Christoph Bezemek*, Freie Meinungsäußerung: Strukturfragen des Schutzbereichs im Rechtsvergleich zwischen dem Ersten Zusatz zur US Verfassung und Artikel 10 EMRK (Verlag Österreich 2015).

[10] See in this regard, for example *Maria Bertel*, Multi-level governance in Südamerika: Das Dezentralisationsmodell der peruanischen Verfassung (Facultas Publishing/Nomos Publishing 2013).

[11] See e.g. *Anna Gamper*, 'Non-cosmopolitan, but Europe-friendly: The Constitutional Court's Comparative Approach' in Tania Groppi, Marie-Claire Ponthoreau (eds.), The Use of Foreign Precedents by Constitutional Judges (Hart Publishing 2013) 213–228; *Anna Gamper*, 'Foreign Precedents in Austrian Constitutional Litigation' (2015) 9 ICL Journal 27–40.

[12] See e.g. *Sebastian M Spitra*, 'Wie kolonial ist Österreichs Rechtsgeschichte? Annäherungen an ein wenig erschlossenes Forschungsfeld' (2021) juridikum 494–502.

[13] *Walter Sauer*, 'Habsburg Colonial: Austria-Hungary's Role in European Overseas Expansion Reconsidered' (2012) 20 Austrian Studies 5, 7–11.

[14] See, in this regard, for example *Daniel Laqua*, The Age of Internationalism and Belgium, 1880–1930: Peace, Progress and Prestige (MUP 2013) 56–64; *Sebastian Conrad*, German Colonialism: A Short History (CUP 2012).

pean countries and the Empire was lacking a significant navy. Discovery trips led to nowhere (e.g. Franz-Joseph's Land in the Artic).[15] As part of a European Alliance against the Boxer Rebellion in China the Austrian-Hungarian Empire gained a very small concession.

To see a bigger involvement of Austria in colonialism, it is necessary to go even further back in time and to include the reign of the House of Habsburg in Spain or in the Netherlands. There is a saying in Austria that Charles V. (House of Habsburg, 16th century) had an "empire, where the sun never set"[16]. This saying referred to the fact that Charles V. was not only the emperor of Austria as well as of the "Holy Roman Emperor", but also King of Spain and the Netherlands.[17] He was responsible for the cruel destruction of native American culture in South America in the first half of the 16th century.[18]

Besides the failed colonialist attempts, the Austrian Empire still has to be understood as an imperialistic regime, which suppressed neighbouring countries over centuries.[19] Moreover, the reigning Habsburgian family was part of a European elite, which followed colonialist approaches around the world.

2. Development cooperation

In contrast to this past, Austria in the 21st century is part of the European Union and understands itself as a country open to the international world. It is export-oriented[20] and commercialises its (monarchical) past for tourism. While the capital city of Vienna is the seat of many international organisations,[21] the Austrian Development Agency (of the Federal Ministry of Foreign Affairs) is underfunded,[22] supporting some African countries like Ethiopia, Uganda, Burkina Faso

---

[15] But see, regarding the involvement of "Austrian" explorers in Africa, *Walter Sauer*, 'Habsburg Colonial: Austria-Hungary's Role in European Overseas Expansion Reconsidered' (2012) 20 Austrian Studies 5.

[16] See, in this regard, for example *Martin Mutschlechner*, 'Karl V.: Das Reich, in dem die Sonne nie unterging' (Die Welt der Habsburger): https://www.habsburger.net/de/kapitel/karl-v-das-reich-dem-die-sonne-nie-unterging accessed 25 August 2025; but see regarding Austrian links to Mexico in the second half of the 19th century *David Pruonto*, 'Did the Second Mexican Empire under Maximilian of Habsburg (1864–1867) have an "Austrian Face"?' (2012) 20 Austrian Studies 96–111.

[17] See *William Maltby*, The Reign of Charles V (Palgrave 2002).

[18] See *William Maltby*, The Rise and Fall of the Spanish Empire (Penguin Books 2008).

[19] The Austrian-Hungarian Empire collapsed after the first world war, which lead to the establishment of various countries in Central and Eastern Europe.

[20] See *Robert Stehrer* and *Roman Stöllinger*, Positioning Austria in the Global Economy: Value Added Trade, International Production Sharing and Global Linkages, FIW-Research Reports No. 2013/14–02, https://www.econstor.eu/handle/10419/121230 accessed 25 August 2025.

[21] E.g. the United Nations, the OSCE or the OPEC.

[22] *APA*, 'Ausgaben für Entwicklungshilfe in Österreich gesunken' (Der Standard 11 April 2024) https://www.derstandard.at/story/3000000215516/oecd-weit-mehr-entwicklungshilfe-in-214sterreich-gesunken accessed 25 August 2025.

or Mozambique.[23] Other rich countries like Norway (1.09 %), Luxembourg (0.99%), Sweden (0.91%), Germany (0.79%) or Denmark (0.74 %)[24] invest much more than Austria (0.38%) in development cooperation.

The Austrian success of a development cooperation with Bhutan led to an end of this cooperation,[25] which, however, also included a collaboration with the first, in 2015 established law school in Thimphu, Buthan's capital.[26] Learning from the Bhutanese approach towards constitution law (see e.g. happiness index[27]) was never seriously discussed in Austria.[28]

Bringing the historical and the actual developments together, it can be seen that the Austrian attitude is very much influenced by an overall European approach towards the Global South. Still without direct colonial experience, Austrian politics primarily operates on a one-way basis. For example, it wants to export products globally and sell the image of Austria as a country with nice mountains and a long-standing tradition in culture and music. A truly intercultural exchange is not part of this perspective. Austrian legal culture does not significantly deviate from this overall approach.[29]

III. Austrian lessons to be learned from the Global South[30]

The following paper tries to identify the possibilities of lessons from the Global South to be drawn for the Global North from an Austrian perspective. As a

---

[23] 'Länder & Regionen' (*Austrian Development Agency)* https://www.entwicklung.at/laender accessed 25 August2025.

[24] Austrian development cooperation 0.38 % of Gross National Income, while the UN target is 0.7 %, see https://www.oecd.org/en/data/indicators/net-oda.html accessed 25 August 2025.

[25] See 'Bhutan (Bis 2023)' (*Austrian Development Agency)* https://www.entwicklung.at/laender/bhutan accessed25 August 2025.

[26] See 'Teaching exchange with the Jigme Singye Wangchuck School of Law' https://asianlaw.univie.ac.at/projects/bhutan/ accessed 22 November 2024 and 'Publications' (*University of Vienna*) https://asianlaw.univie.ac.at/projects/publications/ accessed25 August 2025.

[27] See Art. 9 para 2 Buthan Constitution 2008: "The State shall strive to promote those conditions that will enable the pursuit of Gross National Happiness." Günter Frankenberg, however, views this regulation as a cultural oddity and argues in the context of the country's poverty that it "comes under the rubric of constitutional deceit [...] and should not be assessed in a too felicitous manner". See *Günter Frankenberg*, Comparative Constitutional Studies: Between Magic and Deceit (Edward Elgar Publishing 2019) 141.

[28] In that regard it might be interesting to know that Vienna is seen as one of the most liveable cities of the world; see, in this regard, 'The Global Liveability Index 2024' (*The Economist*) https://www.eiu.com/n/campaigns/global-liveability-index-2024/ accessed25 August 2025; however, Viennese people traditionally have also been understood as grumpy people.

[29] See *Konrad Lachmayer* and *Niklas Sonntag*, 'An Introduction to Austrian Legal Culture' in Sören Koch and Marius Mikkel Kjølstad (eds.), Handbook on Legal Cultures: A Selection of the World's Legal Cultures (Springer Publishing 2023) 75–105.

[30] The paper does not contribute to the debate about the concept of Global South. In that regard see *Philipp Dann* "Southern Lessons for Constitutional Law – A view from Germany".

starting point, Austrian Constitutionalism and its struggles shall be introduced (B.). Based on these deficits of Austrian constitutional law, contents will be discussed, on how concepts of the Global South can improve Austrian constitutionalism in the 21st century (C.). Following this substantive approach, opportunities (D.) and challenges (E.) will be identified to go on with such an approach. The paper ends with general conclusions on how European countries might adopt a truly global approach towards constitutionalism in the 21st century (F.).

B. 100 years of Austrian Constitutionalism

I. The Constitution of 1920

The Austrian Constitution of 1920 is known as the work of Hans Kelsen, the founding father of this constitution.[31] In 2020, Austria officially celebrated the 100th anniversary of its constitution,[32] especially with its model of a specialised constitutional court.[33] The Austrian Constitution of 1920, however, failed in two aspects to fulfil its claim of addressing the core constitutional issues. On the one hand, it could not provide a constitutional concept of the allocation of powers between the federation and the states, on the other hand, the dominant parties (conservative party and social democratic party) could not agree on social rights.[34] While it was possible to agree on an allocation of powers in 1925 (due to

[31] Ewald Wiederin argues that Hans Kelsen has to be understood much more as a founding mother instead of founding father of the Austrian Constitution; see *Ewald Wiederin*, 'Der österreichische Verfassungsgerichtshof als Schöpfung Hans Kelsens und sein Modellcharakter als eigenständiges Verfassungsgericht' in Thomas Simon and Johannes Kalwoda (eds.), Schutz der Verfassung: Normen, Institutionen, Höchst- und Verfassungsgerichte (Duncker & Humblot 2014) 283, 306 ("As editor of the Constitution, he has carried out the concept of the constitutional court and as a constitutional judge he nurtured it in its critical early years, as a constitutional years, and as a constitutional theorist he defended it against all attacks, both unjustified and justified").

[32] However, it only has been 88 years since the Austrian Constitution came into force. In times of Austrian fascism and subsequent national socialism, the Constitution of 1920 was not in force from 1933 to 1945. It was then reinstated in the version of 1929; see e.g. *Alexander Somek*, 'Authoritarian Constitutionalism: Austrian Constitutional Doctrine 1933 to 1938 and Its Legacy' in Christian Joerges and Navraj Singh Ghaleigh (eds.), The Darker Legacies of Law in Europe: The Shadow of National Socialism and Fascism over Europe and its Legal Traditions (Bloomsbury Publishing 2003) 361–388.

[33] Austria is proud of the Austrian model of constitutional adjudication; see e.g. *Verfassungsgerichtshof*, 100 Jahre Verfassungsgerichtshof 1920–2020 (Publishing Österreich 2021); see regarding the forgotten roots of the Austrian model of constitutional adjudication *Ewald Wiederin*, Vergessene Wurzeln der konzentrierten Normenkontrolle in Österreich (Verlag Österreich 2021).

[34] See *Manfred Stelzer*, The Constitution of the Republic of Austria: A Contextual Analysis (2nd edn, Hart Publishing 2022) 195.

huge international economic pressure),[35] the Austrian Constitution adopted (as a compromise) the old fundamental rights catalogue of 1867, which only contained civil liberties (and no social rights).

From 2003 to 2005 the Austrian Convention was held to fundamentally renew the Austrian Constitution.[36] This included the development of a new and coherent catalogue on human and fundamental rights, which Austria had been lacking until then. Once again, social rights have proven to be the point of conflict as the different parties could not agree upon them. In the end, the whole convention failed, and no new constitution was enacted.[37] While changes were realised in other fields of constitutional law, including a clearing up of constitutional provisions,[38] the introduction of administrative courts of first instance[39] and the establishment of parliamentary committees of inquiry as a right of the parliamentary minority (instead of majority as before),[40] the topic of social rights was never touched upon afterwards. As described in the introductory example, the possibility of the implementation of social rights was called into question. An argument of the existence and application of social rights outside Europe was never made.

II. The constitutional approach towards international law

Anna Gamper illustrates in her paper on "Foreign Precedents in Austrian Constitutional Litigation"[41] that the Austrian Constitutional Court is Europe-friendly but not cosmopolitan.[42] While the Court regularly refers to decisions of the CJEU and the ECtHR, the Court "almost exclusively refers to German courts";[43] also an implicit use of foreign precedents would particularly concern German constitutional case law.[44] Although the Austrian Constitutional Court is considered to be open to European and international law, it followed a different approach concerning environmental constitutionalism.

---

[35] Ibid. 147.

[36] See 'Österreich Konvent' www.konvent.gv.at accessed25 August 2025.

[37] *Harald Eberhard* and *Konrad Lachmayer*, 'Constitutional Reform 2008 in Austria' (2008) 2 ICL Journal 112, 117–118.

[38] See *Harald Eberhard* and *Konrad Lachmayer*, 'Accountability Constitutional Reform and Minority Rights' (2008) 2 ICL Journal 76.

[39] Federal Law Gazette I 51/2012.

[40] Federal Law Gazette I 5/2024.

[41] See *Anna Gamper*, 'Foreign Precedents in Austrian Constitutional Litigation' (2015) 9 ICL Journal 27, 29–32.

[42] *Konrad Lachmayer* and *Niklas Sonntag*, 'An Introduction to Austrian Legal Culture' in Sören Koch and Marius Mikkel Kjølstad (eds.), Handbook on Legal Cultures: A Selection of the World's Legal Cultures (Springer Publishing 2023) 75–105.

[43] *Anna Gamper*, 'Foreign Precedents in Austrian Constitutional Litigation' (2015) 9 ICL Journal 27, 31.

[44] Ibid. 36.

The ACC case concerning a third runway at the Vienna airport in 2017 was crucial in that regard.[45] The Federal Administrative Court of First Instance declined the application of the Vienna airport company to establish a third runway due to environmental reasons, especially taking climate change into consideration. The ACC, however, overturned the decision by not only declaring the judgment of the Federal Administrative Court as arbitrary, but it even went further and rejected all – to a certain extent in its own case law existing – approaches towards environmental constitutionalism. Since then, the ACC was not able to properly address the issue of climate change at all. While the climate change decision of the German Federal Constitutional Court (FCC) from 2021 is understood as groundbreaking,[46] the ACC fell behind.[47] As the argumentation of the FCC is not open to the ACC with regard to the case law of 2017, the Court could adopt an approach which refers to the case law of the ECtHR concerning Art. 8 ECHR in the case on senior women for climate protection in Switzerland (Schweizer KlimaSeniorinnen)[48].

III. Transparency

Based on a global ranking with regard to the right to information, Austria was ranked one of the last positions in the world.[49] The reason for that is that until the year 2025, Austrian constitutional law did not provide a general right to freedom of information, especially no general access to governmental information.[50] The Constitution was still based on a centuries old concept of bureaucracy, which was founded in official secrecy instead of transparency. Austrian governments over the past 15 years failed to establish a new concept of transparency including a Freedom of Information Act (FOIA).[51] The corresponding amendment to the

---

[45] Austrian Constitutional Court, 29.06.2017, E 875/2017.

[46] Federal Constitutional Court of Germany, 24.03.2021, 1 BvR 2656/18.

[47] *Konrad Lachmayer*, 'The Constitutional Context of Climate Change Litigation: A comparative analysis of Germany and Austria' in Ivano Alogna and others (eds.), Climate Change Litigation in Europe: Comparative & Sectoral Perspectives and the Way Forward (Intersentia Publishing 2024) 59–78.

[48] See ECtHR, 09.04.2024, 53600/20, Verein Klimaseniorinnen Schweiz and other v. Switzerland.

[49] See 'The RTI Rating analyses the quality of the world's access to information laws' https://www.rti-rating.org/ accessed 22 November 2024. This changed in 2025.

[50] However, the Austrian constitution previously also provided for a restricted right to information, but only for individuals with a specific legal interest.

[51] Interestingly enough, the constitutional law changed by the development of new case law of the ECtHR concerning Art. 10 ECHR (freedom of expression). As the ECtHR acknowledged the importance of social watchdogs in a democracy, the Court granted further freedom of information rights to this group of society. As the ECHR is part of Austrian constitutional law, the ACC heavily refers to the ECHR and the case law of the ECtHR. Nevertheless, the old provision concerning official secrecy (Art. 20 para 3 F-CA) remained unchanged for a very long time.

Austrian Constitution was finally adopted in 2024[52] and enteredinto force on 1 September 2025.

Due to an ongoing politicisation of the Austrian Federal Ministerial Administration in the last 20 years and further attempts of populist governments to increase political pressure on the bureaucracy, the problems of corruption multiplied.[53] The structural deficits of the constitutional framework became more and more visible and finally ended up in the enactment of a FOIA including a constitutional right to freedom of information.[54] The constitutional amendment failed to take into consideration any constitutional developments occurring outside Europe. If it took other countries into consideration, the relevance of the German legal order can be mentioned.[55]

IV. Interim résumé

While Austrian scholars are proud to show the interesting and innovative elements of the Austrian Constitution and its importance in the development of constitutionalism globally, the downsides and pitfalls of Austrian constitutional law are typically not addressed. As demonstrated in this section of the paper, it can be seen that there is still quite a room for improvement regarding the Austrian Constitution. While Austrian constitutional law, practice and scholarship is reluctant to look beyond the European horizon, more interesting developments regarding the flaws of the Austrian Constitutions could be identified in the Global South. This seems to be a good starting point for learning lessons from other constitutions,[56] which does not only refer to constitutional law in a European but also a global perspective.

---

[52] Federal Law Gazette I 5/2024.

[53] *Kevin Hinterberger* and *Konrad Lachmayer*, 'Challenges of liberal democracy in Austria: Lessons Learned from Current Government Crises' in Bertrand Mathieu and Georges Katrougalos (eds.), The Crisis of Liberal Democracy: Diagnostics and Therapies (Intersentia Publishing 2023) 127–138.

[54] The Austrian Constitution was amended (Federal Law Gazette I 5/2024) and a new Art. 22a F-CA introduces the right to freedom of information, especially a right of access to (governmental) information, on a constitutional level. The amendment will enter into force on 1 September 2025.

[55] See *Konrad Lachmayer*, 'Eine Sprache, zwei Rechtskulturen: deutsches und österreichisches Verfassungsrechtsdenken' in Uwe Kischel (ed.), Der Einfluss des deutschen Verfassungsrechtsdenkens in der Welt: Bedeutung, Grenzen, Zukunftsperspektiven (Mohr Siebeck Publishing 2014) 65–91.

[56] See regarding a functionalist approach in comparative constitutional law *Mark Tushnet*, 'Comparative Constitutional Law' in Mathias Reimann and Reinhard Zimmermann (eds.), The Oxford Handbook of Comparative Law (2nd edn, OUP 2019) 1193–1221; *Vicki C. Jackson*, 'Comparative Constitutional Law: Methodologies' in Michel Rosenfeld and András Sajó (eds.), The Oxford Handbook of Comparative Constitutional Law (OUP 2012) 54–74.

C. Contents

I. A View around the world

In examining the illustrated examples of Austrian deficits, it is fruitful to look beyond Europe and to identify potential learnings. One advantage of this approach is that you could find a multitude of constitutions and constitutional traditions younger than the Austrian ones.[57] The experiences and social problems from other parts of the world might differ significantly from Austria.[58] Nevertheless, it provides a rich set of concepts and understandings, which might be overlooked in the Austrian debate. Learnings from other legal orders – and this is a general challenge in comparative law – cannot be applied in exactly the same manner, but have to be adapted to the particular legal order.[59]

In that regard classic examples from the Global South[60] shall give first insights in possible learnings for Austria. The paper will focus on social rights (II.1.), nature rights and sustainability (II.2.) as well as the topic of the (new) fourth branch (II.3.). There, however, are many more examples, which cannot be discussed here. These include the role of cities in constitutional law, which is traditionally weakened by federalism in Austria,[61] or the role of social media concerning hate speech. In the latter context, the developments around the shutdown of X (former Twitter)[62] lead to a new direction in restricting freedom of speech concerning the non-compliance of international social media corporations.[63]

---

[57] See part D.

[58] See part E.

[59] See *Uwe Kischel*, Rechtsvergleichung (C.H. Beck Publishing 2015) 92–164.

[60] Understanding the Global South by referring to classic examples also includes a certain bias, which cannot be resolved in this paper.

[61] See *Ran Hirschl*, City, State: Constitutionalism and the Megacity (OUP 2020); see *Konrad Lachmayer*, 'Empowering Cities by Constitutional Pluralism' in Richard Albert, Alexandra Flynn and Nathalie Des Rosiers (eds.), The Past, Present, and Future of Canadian Cities: Where the Law Went Wrong and How We Can Fix It (McGill-Queen's University Press 2024) 229–250.

[62] See *Julia Vargas Jones*, 'Elon Musk bows to pressure from Brazil's top court in a bid to reinstate X', CNN 23.9.2024, https://edition.cnn.com/2024/09/23/tech/elon-musk-brazil-court-compliance/index.html accessed 25 August 2025.

[63] See the Case of the Austrian Supreme Court, 15.9.2020, 6 Ob 195/19y with regard to a Worldwide Obligation of Facebook to Cease and Desist from the Publication of Photographs of Dr. Eva Glawischnig-Piesczek in Connection with Defamatory Insults and/or Words of Equivalent Meaning (see https://www.ogh.gv.at/en/uncategorized/worldwide-obligation-of-facebook-to-cease-and-desist-from-the-publication-of-photographs-of-dr-eva-glawischnig-piesczek-in-connection-with-defamatory-insults-and-or-words-of-equivalent-meaning/ accessed25 August 2025).

II. Examples

1. Social rights

Social rights catalogues can nowadays be found in many countries around the world.[64] Certain jurisdictions have developed significant case law in that regard, e.g. India, South Africa and Colombia. Courts in these three legal orders were able to develop social rights further or extend the scope of social rights.[65] This does not mean that the case law has always been without significant restraints and conflicts, but the apex courts developed relevant human rights jurisdiction within their constitutional order,[66] which are of crucial importance to other countries like Austria.

Their case law shows how to operationalise social rights,one of the major concerns in Austria. A good example refers to the right to health, as it is not established in Austrian constitutional law[67] andwas of particular interest in times of the COVID-19 crisis.[68] While the Indian Supreme Court illustrated how to derive a right to health from the right to life,[69] the Colombian Constitutional Court exemplifies that it is even possible to establish concrete support for the people if the legislator and the governmentare not willing to do so. Although

---

[64] *David S. Law* and *Mila Versteeg*, 'The Evolution and Ideology of Global Constitutionalism' (2011) 99 California Law Review 1163, 1194–1202.

[65] *Katharine G Young*, Constituting Economic and Social Rights (OUP 2012) 82–87, 196–206.

[66] *Pratap Bhanu Mehta* and *Shylashri Shankar*, 'Courts and Socioeconomic Rights in India' in Varun Gauri and Daniel M Brinks (eds.), Courting Social Justice: Judicial Enforcement of Social and Economic Rights in the Developing World (CUP 2008) 146–182; *Lisa Forman* and *Jerome Amir Singh*, 'The Role of Rights and Litigation in Assuring More Equitable Access to Health Care in South Africa' in Colleen M. Flood and Aeyal Gross (eds.), The Right to Health at the Public/Private Divide (CUP 2014) 288–318; *Everaldo Lamprea*, 'Colombia's Right-to-Health Litigation in a Context of Health Care Reform' in Colleen M. Flood and Aeyal Gross (eds.), The right to health at the public/private divide: A global comparative study (CUP 2014) 131–158.

[67] See *Manfred Stelzer*, The Constitution of the Republic of Austria. A Contextual Analysis (2nd edn, Hart Publishing 2022) 195; *Konrad Lachmayer*, 'Constitutional Compliance or Governmental Mismanagement? Rights Limitations in Austria from Lockdowns to Compulsory Vaccination' in Arianna Vedaschi (ed.), Government Policies to Fight Pandemics: Defining the Boundaries of Legitimate Limitations on Fundamental Freedoms (Brill 2024) 115–136.

[68] *Konrad Lachmayer*, 'Democracy, Death and Dying: The Potential and Limits of Legal Rationalisation' in Matthias C. Kettemann and Konrad Lachmayer (eds.), Pandemocracy in Europe: Power, Parliaments and People in Times of COVID-19 (Hart Publishing 2022) 47, 60–61.

[69] *Pratap Bhanu Mehta* and *Shylashri Shankar*, 'Courts and Socioeconomic Rights in India' in Varun Gauri and Daniel M Brinks (eds.), Courting Social Justice: Judicial Enforcement of Social and Economic Rights in the Developing World (CUP 2008) 146–182.

some might viewthe Colombian example as deterrent, it can also be understood as a way to make social rights enforceable.[70]

The Austrian debate by confronting itself with the global experiences could learn that the operationalisation of social rights is possible,[71] and that different approaches can be followed. The argument that we do not need social rights as the social state works well falls short, as this would apply to liberal rights and the rule of law in the same manner. On the contrary, it is better to establish social rights in times when the social security system is still functioning well. This would enable preparation for periods of increased pressure on the social system.[72]

2. Sustainability

Austria, a country largely covered by the Alpes, will lose its last glaciers in the next 50 years.[73] In that regard it is remarkable that the Indian High Court of the State Uttarakhand argued in 2017 in favour of legal personhood of glaciers and rivers.[74]

In a more general manner, the Constitution of Ecuador was amended in 2008 to implement nature rights into constitutional law.[75] These rights include the rights of the nature to "integral respect for its existence and for the maintenance and regeneration of its life cycles, structure, functions and evolutionary processes" (Art. 71) and the "right to be restored" (Art. 72). All "[p]ersons, communities, peoples, and nations shall have the right to benefit from the environment

[70] *Everaldo Lamprea*, 'Colombia's Right-to-Health Litigation in a Context of Health Care Reform' in Colleen M. Flood and Aeyal Gross (eds.), The right to health at the public/private divide: A global comparative study (CUP 2014) 131–158.

[71] See *Dragana Damjanovic*, 'Soziale Grundrechte' in Gregor Heißl (ed.), Handbuch Menschenrechte, Allgemeine Grundlagen – Grundrechte in Österreich – Entwicklungen – Rechtsschutz (Facultas Publishing 2009) 516–532.

[72] *Karl Stöger*, 'Austria: Legal Response to Covid-19' in Jeff King, Octávio Ferraz and others (eds.), The Oxford Compendium of National Legal Responses to Covid-19 (OUP 2021) doi: 10.1093/law-occ19/e28.013.28; *Konrad Lachmayer*, 'Constitutional Compliance or Governmental Mismanagement? Rights Limitations in Austria from Lockdowns to Compulsory Vaccination' in Arianna Vedaschi (ed.), Government Policies to Fight Pandemics: Defining the Boundaries of Legitimate Limitations on Fundamental Freedoms (Brill 2024) 115–136.

[73] See
https://infothek.bmimi.gv.at/gletscherbericht-alpenverein-oesterreich-in-40-bis-45-jahren-eisfrei/accessed25 August 2025.

[74] See the High Court of Utterakhand at Nainital, 30.3.2017, Lalit Miglani vs State Of Uttarakhand And Others, MCC 139/2017, CLMA 2359/2017 the Supreme Court of India has suspended the judgement (Supreme Court of India, 'Daily Cause List Dated: 16–12–2019', Items 40 and 40.1, pp. 1–155, at 8.); see Stellina Jolly and K.S. Roshan Menon, 'Of Ebbs and Flows: Understanding the Legal Consequences of Granting Personhood to Natural Entities in India' (2021) 10 Transnational Environmental Law 467, 468.

[75] *Mihnea Tanasescu*, 'The rights of nature in Ecuador: the making of an idea' (2013) 70 International Journal of Environmental Studies 6, 846–861.

and the natural wealth enabling them to enjoy the good way of living" (Art. 74). According to Art. 73, the state "shall apply preventive and restrictive measures on activities that might lead to the extinction of species, the destruction of ecosystems and the permanent alteration of natural cycles."[76]

While the ACC was not able to come up with an active interpretation of the existing state objectives as well as an implementation of European legislation in place concerning environmental protection,[77] a debate on nature rights developed only on an academic level in Austria.[78] However, the environmental threats concerning climate change and the loss of biodiversity are also tremendous in Austria.[79] Many other countries have already begun to follow or at least to discuss these Southern examples of environmental constitutionalism. The Austrian public debate is lagging behind.[80]

3. Fourth Branch

The third example concerns the debates about a fourth branch regarding the safeguards of democracy by introducing certain authorities. When it comes to anti-corruption strategies, the international debate refers, for example, to Brazil and South Africa.[81] While the Brazilian trend is focusing more on practical developments, the South African case concerns questions of constitutional institutions. Chapter 9 of the South African Constitution includes a number of institutions to guard democracy, including the Public Prosecutor, the Human Rights Commission, the Auditor-General and the independent Electoral Authority. These institutions, especially the Public Prosecutor, played a significant role in the fight against corruption in South Africa.[82]

In recent years, the fight against high-level corruption in Austria has involved both politics and the legal system on a tremendous scale.[83] This involved the

---

[76] See *Louis J. Kotzé* and *Paola Villavicencio Villavicencio*, 'Somewhere between Rhetoric and Reality: Environmental Constitutionalism and the Rights of Nature in Ecuador' (2017) 6 Transnational Environmental Law 401–433.

[77] See above, B.II.

[78] See e.g. *Tina Rametsteiner*, Rechte der Natur. Eine rechtsvergleichende Untersuchung unter besonderer Berücksichtigung der 'Rechte von Flüssen' (Duncker & Humblot 2025).

[79] See *BMK* (ed.), Klimawandelanpassung und Biodiversität. Anpassung an den Klimawandel geht mit Naturschutz Hand in Hand (2022) https://www.bmk.gv.at/dam/jcr:d879e03a-a6ea-433b-a5e3-9d4be49f2e88/Publikation_Biodiversitaet_A5_12-2022.pdf accessed 22 November 2024.

[80] See *Daniel Ennöckl* (ed.), Klimaschutzrecht (Verlag Österreich 2023).

[81] *Mark Tushnet*, A New Fourth Branch: Institutions for Protecting Constitutional Democracy (CUP 2021) 97–123.

[82] See *Lauren Kohn*, 'The National Prosecuting Authority as Part of South Africa's Integrity and Accountability Branch and the Related Case for an Anti-Corruption Redress System' (2022) 12 Constitutional Court Review 1–58.

[83] *Kevin Hinterberger* and *Konrad Lachmayer*, 'Challenges of liberal democracy in Austria: Lessons Learned from Current Government Crises' in Bertrand Mathieu and Georges Ka-

Public Prosecutor's Office as well as Parliamentary Committees of Inquiries. The constitutional law was amended in favour of both institutions in the last 20 years.[84] The situation escalated to such an extend that the Austrian Constitutional Court had to initiate an enforcement procedure of its own judgement, as the Ministry of Finance was not willing to comply (to hand over a huge amount of information to Parliament).[85]

The Austrian debate did not acknowledge the international debate about the fourth branch of government. In that regard, the existing constitutional amendments were never understood in the context of fighting corruption and the current situation is not reflecting the collaboration of the two institutions (Parliamentary Committees and the Public Prosecutor) in the context of anti-corruption. Nevertheless, the Austrian constitutional debate and scholarship could learn a lot from the experience in the South. It would even be possible to amend the constitution in this respect in order to expand the powers of these institutions concerning the field of anti-corruption.[86] A major concern is the dependence of the Public Prosecutor on the Minister of Justice,[87] which could be discussed differently in the context of a fourth branch thinking of the institution safeguarding democracy.

III. Interim résumé

The three examples show the potential of constitutional learning from the South from an Austrian perspective. There are many constitutional issues waiting to be resolved and trapped in an Austrian constitutional debate. In contrast, the examples demonstrate the rich plurality of potential ways to adapt Austrian constitutionalism. They concern possible constitutional amendments as well as constitutional interpretation by the Austrian Constitutional Court.

While the chosen examples focus on possibilities on how to improve constitutional law and constitutionalism in Austria, it shall not be ignored that also negative developments and the way of constitutional decline might be of rel-

---

trougalos (eds.), The Crisis of Liberal Democracy: Diagnostics and Therapies (Intersentia Publishing 2023) 127–138.

[84] Federal Law Gazette I 2/2008 (shifting the Public Prosecutors Office from the executive branch to the judicial branch); Federal Law Gazette I 101/2014 (enabling the establishment of parliamentary committees of inquiry for a 25% minority in the parliament instead of a majority of the parliament).

[85] *Konrad Lachmayer*, 'An Austrian Abyss of Cronyism and Corruption: Fighting for the Rule of Law in Austria' (2021) VerfBlog, https://verfassungsblog.de/an-austrian-abyss-of-cronyism-and-corruption/, DOI: 10.17176/20210602–003917–0 accessed25 August 2025.

[86] The establishment of judicial investigation bodies concerning governmental misconduct to defend democracy like in South Africa is not possible in Austria.

[87] *Klaus Schwaighofer*, 'The public prosecutor in Austria' (2024) 62 DPCE Online 387–405.

evance in comparative law. In that regard, it is also necessary to learn for times of emergency[88] and regarding pressure on constitutional law.[89]

The value of comparative law is not limited to certain inspirations; it also serves the purpose of widening the perspective and to learn from other countries. On the one hand, the examples illustrate the extensive scope of topics and possibilities to reflect and improve Austrian constitutional law by learning from the Global South. On the other hand, the presented examples in this paper can only give a superficial insight into the constitutional orders concerned. The deeper challenges to comparative constitutional law with the Global South could not be addressed properly regarding the mentioned examples.

D. Opportunities

I. Theoretical potential

1. Learnings ...

Comparative constitutional law can be defined as a process of learning from one another.[90] Functionalism argues in favour of learning from other countries, while limiting the group of relevant legal orders to those with basic similarities (presumption of similarity).[91] Critics of learning from other countries argue that each individual country has its own particular legal culture and that it is not possible to transfer legal concepts.[92] Nevertheless, it seems possible to claim that "the field [of

[88] See *Konrad Lachmayer*, 'Constitutional Compliance or Governmental Mismanagement? Rights Limitations in Austria from Lockdowns to Compulsory Vaccination' in Arianna Vedaschi (ed.), Government Policies to Fight Pandemics: Defining the Boundaries of Legitimate Limitations on Fundamental Freedoms (Brill 2024) 115–136.

[89] Challenges of populism also exist in Austria, see *Konrad Lachmayer*, 'Questioning the Basic Values I – Austria and Jörg Haider' in András Jakab and Dimitry Kochenov (eds.), The Enforcement of EU Law and Values: Ensuring Member States' Compliance (OUP 2017) 436–455; *Konrad Lachmayer*, 'Formalism and Judicial Self-Restraint as Tools Against Populism? Considerations regarding Recent Developments of the Austrian Constitutional Court' in Fruszina Gárdos-Orosz and Zoltán Szente (eds.), Populist Challenges to Constitutional Interpretation in Europe and Beyond (Routledge Publishing 2021) 75–94; *Kevin Hinterberger* and *Konrad Lachmayer*, 'Challenges of liberal democracy in Austria. Lessons Learned from Current Government Crises' in Bertrand Mathieu and Georges Katrougalos (eds.), The Crisis of Liberal Democracy. Diagnostics and Therapies (Intersentia Publishing 2023) 127–138.

[90] This is reflected by a traditional functionalist approach: see *Vicki C. Jackson*, 'Comparative Constitutional Law: Methodologies' in Michel Rosenfeld and András Sajó (eds.), The Oxford Handbook of Comparative Constitutional Law (OUP Press 2012) 54, 62–66.

[91] *Ralf Michaels*, 'The Functional Method of Comparative Law' in Mathias Reimann and Reinhard Zimmermann (eds.), The Oxford Handbook of Comparative Law (2nd edn, OUP 2019) 345, 375.

[92] *Pierre Legrand*, Negative Comparative Law. A Strong Programme for Weak Thought (CUP 2022).

comparative law] requires non-Eurocentric critiques of Eurocentrism and of non-Eurocentrism alike".[93]

Learning from other legal orders, especially in the context of constitutional law, has also been under critique[94] as it seemed to be a one-way road from Western legal order to the rest of the world. This also included a one-dimensional export from bigger to smaller countries. Moreover, there is a specific element to this Western dominance, especially that of the most influential constitutional orders of Germany and the United States[95] in constitutional law, but also of the French and the British legal order[96] which must also address the post-colonial realities of the Global South.[97] The post-colonial situation does not only concern the Global South but also the former colonisers themselves.

If one leaves a harmonising understanding of learning and follows a more reciprocal approach from an epistemological perspective, learning can enable an equal exchange between different constitutional orders, without giving one a conceptual or epistemic supremacy over the other.[98] In this regard, learning is neither limited to constitutional orders, which derive from the same legal tradition, nor is it looking for a dominant legal order. It only depends on the question of what a constitutional order has to offer in terms of potential inspiration regarding meanings or interpretation of constitutional concepts to another country.[99] The specific interrelation between the two constitutional orders compared becomes relevant. The problem or challenges, which occurred in one constitutional order, and the potential solutions to these problems offered by another constitutional order have to fit together to create a space for learning (in the best case from each other). A deeper engagement in learning from another constitutional order makes it necessary to have a closer look at the context.[100]

When accepting that the learning paradigm is a legitimate approach in comparative law in general, it is important to have a closer look at what can be

---

[93] Ibid., 217.

[94] See *Günter Frankenberg*, Comparative Constitutional Studies: Between Magic and Deceit (Edward Elgar Publishing 2019) 81–85.

[95] See *Uwe Kischel* (ed.), Der Einfluss des deutschen Verfassungsrechtsdenkens in der Welt: Bedeutung, Grenzen, Zukunftsperspektiven (Mohr Siebeck Publishing 2014); *David S. Law* and *Mila Versteeg*, 'The Declining Influence of the United States Constitution' (2012) 87 N.Y.U. L. Rev. 762–858.

[96] This relates to the British and French colonialism.

[97] See e.g. regarding the negation of liberal constitutionalism in the post-colonial Africa *Berihun Adugna Gebeye*, A Theory of African Constitutionalism (OUP 2021) 58–63.

[98] *Philipp Dann*, *Michael Riegner* and *Maxim Bönnemann*, 'The Southern Turn in Comparative Constitutional Law' in Philipp Dann, Michael Riegner and Maxim Bönnemann (eds.), The Global South and Comparative Constitutional Law, Oxford Comparative Constitutionalism (OUP 2020) 3.

[99] *Mark Tushnet*, 'The Possibilities of Comparative Constitutional Law' (1999) 108 Yale LJ 1226–1309.

[100] See *Uwe Kischel*, Comparative Law (OUP 2019) 152–188.

learned from other constitutional orders. As constitutional law concerns the fundamental rules and principles of a legal order as well as it deals with fundamental values, especially in the context of human rights, the fields of comparison have proven to be broad and manifold. The potential to learn more about these issues and identify more interesting topics is also linked to the selections of constitutional orders involved. Opening up this perspective creates a significant potentialfor the search of new approaches that have not yet been considered.[101]

2. ... *from the Global South*

While a traditional approach offered the Global South the possibility to learn from the Global North, a shift can be observed in the last decades.[102] The change started by strengthening the exchange between different constitutional orders of the Global South to learn from each other (e.g. in Africa or between Latin America and Africa).[103] As the idea and the concept of constitutional law was developed in the Global North[104] and exported to the Global South, learnings from the Global South to the North seemed neither relevant nor possible. The developments of the last decades created the potential for a significant shift. Constitutions of the Global North, although they may have been amended several times, as in Austria,[105] or renewed, as in Switzerland,[106] have not been able to respond to the challenges of the 21st century in the same way as the constitutions of the Global South, but have instead followed established concepts within their own legal traditions.

---

[101] See the approach by *David S. Law* (ed.) Constitutionalism in Context (CUP 2022).

[102] *Philipp Dann*, *Michael Riegner* and *Maxim Bönnemann*, 'The Southern Turn in Comparative Constitutional Law' in Philipp Dann, Michael Riegner and Maxim Bönnemann (eds.), The Global South and Comparative Constitutional Law, Oxford Comparative Constitutionalism (OUP 2020) 1.

[103] See regarding the relevance of the Global South in comparative constitutional law *Philipp Dann*, *Michael Riegner* and *Maxim Bönnemann*, 'The Southern Turn in Comparative Constitutional Law' in Philipp Dann, Michael Riegner and Maxim Bönnemann (eds.), The Global South and Comparative Constitutional Law, Oxford Comparative Constitutionalism (OUP 2020) 12–14; *Ran Hirschl*, Comparative Matters: The Renaissance of Comparative Constitutional Law (OUP 2014) 217–223; see examples of South-South comparison e.g. *Anthony C. Diala*, 'Reform of the customary law of inheritance in Nigeria: lessons from South Africa' (2014) 14 African Human Rights Law Journal 2, 633–654; *Jackie Durgard*, 'A View from (South) Africa' in Conrado Hübner Mendes, Roberto Gargarella and Sebastian Guidi (eds.), The Oxford handbook of constitutional law in Latin America (OUP 2022) 849–856.

[104] The spread of constitutional law around the world is part of the post-colonial paradigm, which goes along with revolutions, the establishment of states and legal order on its own.

[105] The Austrian Federal Constitutional Act has been amended more than 130 times since 1945.

[106] See the new Swiss Constitution 1999; *Rene Rhinow*, 'Die Neue Verfassung in der Schweiz' (2002) 41 Der Staat 575–596.

In contrast, constitutions of the Global South have proven to be more innovative and more dynamic.[107] While some constitutional traditionshave existed for a long time,[108] the occurrence of upheavals and the need to restructure in post-colonial times have challenged many societies.[109] These developments increased the potential to pave the way for new constitutional content.

Learning from the Global South creates a potential to draw on a wealth of epistemic experiences. Societal problems, like authoritarianism, social inequalities or dealing with all kinds of crisis (including financial, migration or health crises), have been a topic for many countries in the Global South for a long time.[110] Socio-technological developments or the environmental implications of the climate crisis are further examples of challenges, with which all countries in the world are confronted.[111] The potential for constitutional learning from the Global South with regard to these areas is significant.

II. Practical prospects

While from a theoretical perspective there are already good reasons to engage globally, there are also many practical developments related to globalisation, which make constitutional comparison easier to reach out to the Global South. These possibilities include the availability of information, the ability to communicate, the ability to travel faster and the intensified opportunities for collaboration.

The availability of information changed significantly in the last 20 years. While in the past much information was not available online, today many legal texts, case law and scholarly literature can be found on the internet. This includes online collections such as the constitute project,[112] as well as databases and case

---

[107] See *Ran Hirschl*, Comparative Matters: The Renaissance of Comparative Constitutional Law (OUP 2014) 205–223; *Ran Hirschl*, Constitutional Innovation in Governing the Metropolis: Law, Economics, Politics (OUP 2020) 103–150.

[108] See e.g. a different situation in certain Latin American countries (see *Roberto Gargarella*, Latin American Constitutionalism 1810–2010 (OUP 2013)) as well as long-lasting legal traditions like in India (see *Arun K Thiruvengadam*, The Constitution of India. A Contextual Analysis (Hart Publishing 2017)).

[109] *Berihun Adugna Gebeye*, A Theory of African Constitutionalism (OUP 2021) 58–71.

[110] See e.g. *Alicia Ely Yamin*, 'The Right to Health' in Conrado Hübner Mendes, Roberto Gargarella and Sebastian Guidi (eds.), The Oxford handbook of constitutional law in Latin America (OUP 2022) 758–781; *Daniel M. Brinks*, 'Social Rights Constitutionalism' in Conrado Hübner Mendes, Roberto Gargarella and Sebastian Guidi (eds.), The Oxford handbook of constitutional law in Latin America (OUP 2022) 744–757; *Maria Paula Saffon*, 'Property and Land' in Conrado Hübner Mendes, Roberto Gargarella and Sebastian Guidi (eds.), The Oxford handbook of constitutional law in Latin America (OUP 2022) 578–597.

[111] See above C.II.2.

[112] See 'Constitute: The World's Constitutions to Read, Search, and Compare' https://www.constituteproject.org/ accessed25 August 2025.

law, which are more domestic.[113] Learning from the Global South has become much more accessible than before.

These developments go hand in hand with the ability to communicate. In the last five years, the possibilities for video calls and online conferences with colleagues from around the world increased significantly. Based on and supplementary to the existing texts available online, the comparative dialogue is crucial to better understand the constitutional developments and struggles. Again, communication technologies play an important role for this comparative engagement.

While online interactions are an important part and a good starting point to intensify comparative learning from the South, the ability to travel faster and easier to other countries around the world is just as relevant for a better comparative understanding. A deeper legal as well as cultural understanding of other constitutional orders requires a personal exchange with colleagues from the legal practice and the academic world. Comparative conferences organised by scholarly organisations[114] or e.g. by constitutional courts[115] are an example of face-to-face exchange. Research visits or scholarly collaborationsenable an intensifies acquision of knowledge.

The possibilities of internet research, virtual communication and relatively easy travel create increased opportunities for collaboration. Combining the existing possibilities in an ever-closer world of comparative constitutional studies provides multiple opportunities to engage more and better with the Global South. In that regard, the Global South and the Global North are more closely linked than ever.

From a practical perspective, the particular situation in Austria is especially predestined to create more collaborative efforts. This refers to many organisational issues. Vienna, the capital city of Austria, is already successfully established as a city in which many international organisation having their seats or a branch.[116] As one of the most liveable cities in the world, Vienna is one of the main destinations for (global) conferences.[117] Moreover, Austria is located in central

[113] Especially websites of parliaments and courts as well as online journals and domestic legal databases.

[114] See e.g. the quadrennial IACL World Congress of Constitutional Law or the annual ICON.S Conferences.

[115] See the World Conference on Constitutional Justice as well as the congresses of the Conference of European Constitutional Courts, the Association of Constitutional Courts, the Southern African Judges Commission, the Conference of Constitutional Control Organs of Countries of New Democracy, the Association of Asian Constitutional Courts and Equivalent Institutions, the Union of Arab Constitutional Courts and Councils, the Ibero-American Conference of Constitutional Justice and the Conference of Constitutional Jurisdictions of Africa.

[116] Including the United Nations, the OECD or the OPEC.

[117] See https://b2b.wien.info/en/newsroom/pressservice/conferences-in-2023-597860accessed, 25 August 2025; https://www.advantageaustria.org/my/news/20230602-wien-kongress-stadt-nummer-1.en.html accessed 25 August 2025.

Europe, which means that from a global perspective distances to India, Africa but even South America are relatively favourable. Overall, Austria cannot only serve as a hub for international collaboration but can also profit from global learning itself

In conclusion, there are many reasons to strengthen comparative exchange with the Global South. From both a theoretical and a practical perspective, it seems not only worthwhile but also important to broaden existing perspectives and to gain and engage with comparative knowledge from the Global South. Nevertheless, one might ask about theoretical hurdles and practical problems that could occur and prevent or slow down this engagement.

E. Challenges

I. Theoretical hurdles

From a theoretical perspective of comparative constitutional law, different concerns might arise when undertaking a comparative constitutional study. As a first and main concern, the possibilities for contextual considerations might be questioned. From a traditional perspective one might argue that there are different legal families[118] or from a functionalist perspective that there is no presumption of similarity.[119] One might argue that learning in comparative constitutional law is not possible at all as significant differences have to be acknowledged.[120] All these arguments limit the possibility of including constitutional knowledge from other parts of the world, as differences are too significant.

While it is crucial to take differences concerning legal orders and legal cultures[121] into consideration, it shall also be argued in favour of comparative constitutional learning beyond legal and cultural differences. When it comes to constitutional law, it seems even more challenging to argue in favour of comparative learning at all, as constitutional identity[122] plays a significant role. When consid-

---

[118] See regarding the criticism of Eurocentrism *H. Patrick Glenn*, 'Comparative Legal Families and Comparative Legal Traditions' in Mathias Reimann and Reinhard Zimmermann (eds.), The Oxford Handbook of Comparative Law (2nd edn, OUP 2019) 423, 433–435.

[119] *Ralf Michaels*, 'The Functional Method of Comparative Law' in Mathias Reimann and Reinhard Zimmermann (eds.), The Oxford Handbook of Comparative Law (2nd edn, OUP 2019), 345, 377 argues in favour of a presumption of functional equivalence, which also creates limitations.

[120] *Pierre Legrand*, Negative Comparative Law. A Strong Programme for Weak Thought (CUP 2022) 217–228.

[121] See, in this regard, for example *Sören Koch* and *Marius Mikkel Kjølstad*, 'Combing Diversity and Structure' in Sören Koch and Marius Mikkel Kjølstad (eds.), Handbook on Legal Cultures (2nd edn, Springer Publishing 2023) 1–13.

[122] See, in this regard, for example *Michel Rosenfeld*, The Identity of the Constitutional Subject: Selfhood, Citizenship, Culture, and Community (Routledge Publishing 2009).

ering different constitutional concepts or different constitutional values, it is crucial to understand a particular society and its constitutional order and culture. In this regard, constitutional law especially reflects the history, the politics and the society of a particular country.[123]

Nevertheless, answers to upcoming constitutional questions – and this applies equally toconstitutional amendments or constitutional adjudication – will be easier to find if different concepts and models are taken into consideration. The epistemological function of comparative constitutional studies becomes relevant here. The ability to better reflect one's own constitutional order, especially when differences are greater, remains crucial as the ability to find one's own way of responding to the societal problems. A limitation to certain constitutional orders, which are understood to be similar from the outset, cannot be followed here. There are no convincing reasons to limit the epistemological broadening of perspectives.[124] As already mentioned, the Global South offers a broad set of new, different and innovative approaches regarding manifold topics of constitutional law, which – as illustrated with regard to the Austrian example[125] – can be of high value. Thus, learning starts with the possibility to gain (constitutional) knowledge. This does not only refer to existing knowledge from countries of the Global North but also from the Global South.

The broadening of perspectives concerning constitutional orders for epistemological reasons as well as for practical shall enable to acknowledge alternative concepts. The availability of these concepts does not reduce the challenge of how to deal with constitutional learnings from other countries, regardless of whether they are drawn from the Global South or the Global North. As already mentioned, constitutional law is particularly embedded in the legal culture as well as the historical, political and social context of a country and, thus, expresses in a particular way the identity of a legal and political order. In that regard, constitutional lessons drawn from other countries have to take the original as well as the compared constitutional order into account. Contexts remain relevant.[126] The migration of constitutional ideas has to consider the complexity of the different constitutional orders. When accepting this more general challenge of the comparative endeavour, there remain no relevant reasons for excluding the Global South from comparative constitutional lessons for the Global North.

---

[123] *Vicki C. Jackson*, 'Comparative Constitutional Law: Methodologies' in Michel Rosenfeld and András Sajó (eds.), The Oxford Handbook of Comparative Constitutional Law (OUP 2012) 54, 66–67, 72, who suggests a contextualised functionalism.

[124] Nevertheless, the concrete values at stake might be relevant. While learning how to improve democratic voting systems will not be possible in autocratic countries, which do not provide fair and transparent elections, other constitutional challenges developments might be of relevance.

[125] See above, B.

[126] See *Günter Frankenberg*, Comparative Constitutional Studies: Between Magic and Deceit (Edward Elgar Publishing 2019) 77, 90, who emphases local knowledge and suggests a layered narrative.

One of the peculiarities of the Global South in most of the countries and in most of the constitutional orders concerned refers to the post-colonial setting. Rather than seeing this as an obstacle to learning from the Global South, it can even be understood as an opportunity for the Global North not only to tell its truth but to listen to the truths of others. From a knowledge-based perspective, the particular challenges of the Global South resulting from colonialism led to the creation of more constitutional innovations and more constitutional plurality, which are especially worth exploring.

II. Practical problems

Different practical problems can identified in the context of the comparative study of the Global South. They relate to the general challenges of comparative constitutional studies which also occur in the context of other countries. Therefore, the general problems of comparative constitutional studies need to be addressed.

A first point refers to existing online information, e.g. concerning the constitutional texts or singular case law. The risk of misunderstanding or cherry-picking is very high. It is, thus, necessary to get a deeper understanding of a particular constitutional order. Especially if the overall context is quite different as it usually is concerning constitutional law in the Global South, it is crucial to engage more.

Language barriers are often a practical problem to access other constitutional orders. In post-colonial settings information might still be available in languages of the Global North. Nevertheless, new technologies, especially the use of AI, might create new possibilities of getting access to information of constitutional orders[127] which had not been accessible before due to language barriers. The use of technological tools, however, shall not create the impression that comparative constitutional knowledge can be gained by over-reliance on automated processed translation.[128]

In that regard, a deeper understanding of the contexts of constitutional orders is useful to create a more substantial understanding of the Global South. This concerns questions such as how certain concepts are applied in a particular society, what positive and negative effects discussed in this context, or how courts create or shape certain constitutional ideas. In many cases, constitutional concepts are answers to particular historical, political or social challenges in a society. This deeper understanding of constitutional orders from the Global South

---

[127] *Lutz-Christian Wolff*, 'Artificial Intelligence ante portas: The End of Comparative Law?' (2019) 7 The Chinese Journal of Comparative Law 484; *Han-wei Ho*, *Chung-Chia Huang* and *Yun-chien Chang*, 'Machine-Learning Comparative Law' in Mathias Siems and Po Jen Yap (eds.), Cambridge Handbook of Comparative Law (CUP 2024) 177–208.

[128] See *Irene Rivera-Trigueros*, 'Machine translation systems and quality assessment: a systematic review' (2022) 56(2) Language Resources & Evaluation 593–619.

is only one side of the coin, while the other side refers to the understanding of the underlying context of the respective constitutional order.

The challenges posed to constitutional comparison could lead to the conclusion that the comparative endeavour is not worth pursuing. The arguments laid out here, however, are intended to illustrate that a careful and serious approach towards comparative constitutional studies is possible and capable of addressing the concerns that have been raised. It is necessary to prevent that the concerns raised lead to comparative constitutional lessons being drawn only from the Global North, while the Global South is excluded.

F. Conclusion

I. An epistemological turn?

In the last decade, comparative constitutional law opened up towards an interdisciplinary understanding as comparative constitutional studies.[129] This multidisciplinary approach towards constitutional comparison includes the relevance of an epistemological dimension of constitutional knowledge. Establishing an epistemological approach towards constitutional comparison helps to overcome outdated distinctions of preferred (seemingly superior) and neglected (seemingly inferior) constitutional orders. Gathering constitutional knowledge as well as creating comparative knowledge, however, faces significant epistemological challenges.

Different scholars follow interesting approaches, which can be understood as a development towards a more epistemologically based approach in comparative constitutional studies.

Philipp Dann, Michael Riegner and Maxim Bönnemann claim a need for epistemic reflexivity in comparative constitutional law.[130] This concerns the recognition of epistemic injustices, a multi-perspectivity, which means a de-centring of Euro-American perspectives in a Frankenbergian approach of distancing and differencing,[131] and a relationality, i.e. legal culture understood as an "inherently

[129] See *Ran Hirschl*, Comparative Matters (OUP 2014) 151–191; *Ran Hirschl*, 'From comparative constitutional law to comparative constitutional studies' (2013) 11 International Journal of Constitutional Law 1–12; see also the recently established journal on Comparative Constitutional Studies (Edward Elgar Publishing).

[130] *Philipp Dann*, *Michael Riegner* and *Maxim Bönnemann*, 'The Southern Turn in Comparative Constitutional Law' in Philipp Dann, Michael Riegner and Maxim Bönnemann (eds.), The Global South and Comparative Constitutional Law, Oxford Comparative Constitutionalism (OUP 2020) 31.

[131] *Günter Frankenberg*, 'Critical Comparisons: Re-Thinking Comparative Law' (1985) 26 Harvard International Law Journal 411–455.

hybrid phenomenon marked by conflicts, contradictions, and global entanglements".[132]

A part of this discourse also attempts to address comparative constitutional language, going beyond an English-based understanding of the constitutional knowledge.[133] The linguistic representation of constitutional knowledge crucially effects our understanding of constitutional law and the way of its comparison.

This can be also supported by having a broader interdisciplinary perspective on the topic. Going beyond the traditional understanding of postcolonialism, e.g. Prathama Banerjee reminds us about the "fascinating instances of thinking across traditions for centuries".[134] This "[t]hinking across traditions not only allows us to recover lost and forgotten intellectual cartographies but also helps us carve out thought regions anew."[135]

II. Global constitutional thinking

If one asks for Southern lessons to constitutional law, the answer shows a plurality of topics of constitutional law, which have been established in complex situations in a post-colonial paradigm. The topics can be understood as a reaction to the existing problems of the past, the challenges of the present and the emerging themes of the future. Constitutional law of the South provides answers, which are linked to their constitutional identity, as well as approaches towards constitutional law inspired by the international migration of constitutional ideas.[136] As many of these societies have faced a multitude of serious challenges and crises in the last decades, their constitutional law is highly dynamic and the established concepts vary significantly.

In that regard, there are many things to learn about the Global South as constitutional law and societies of the Global North also have to address many questions and challenges which arose in the 21st century. Many concepts and constitutional "answers" from the 20th century no longer work and new ones have

---

[132] *Philipp Dann*, *Michael Riegner* and *Maxim Bönnemann*, 'The Southern Turn in Comparative Constitutional Law' in Philipp Dann, Michael Riegner and Maxim Bönnemann (eds.), The Global South and Comparative Constitutional Law, Oxford Comparative Constitutionalism (OUP 2020) 33.

[133] See, in this regard, for example *Maartje De Visser*, 'Towards a More Inclusive Constitutional Discourse: Overcoming Linguistic Barriers' (2022) Int'l J. Const. L. Blog, 18 May 2022 https://www.iconnectblog.com/towards-a-more-inclusive-constitutional-discourse-overcoming-linguistic-barriers/ accessed 25 August 2025; *Odile Ammann*, 'English Language Bias in Comparative Constitutional Law Scholarship' in Erika Arban, Maartje De Visser and Jeong-In Yun (eds.), The Language of Comparative Constitutional Law: Questioning Hegemonies (Hart Publishing forthcoming).

[134] *Prathama Banerjee*, Elementary aspects of the political: Histories from the Global South (DUP 2021) 215.

[135] Ibid., 216.

[136] *Sujit Choudhry*, 'Migration as a new metaphor in comparative constitutional law' in Sujit Choudhry (ed.), The Migration of constitutional ideas (CUP 2006) 1, 19–25.

to be developed. In that regard, comparative constitutional studies engaging with the Global South offer inspiration and possible exchanges for the Global North in many respects.

These conclusions also apply to the Austrian constitutional order. Although Austria failed to establish lasting colonialism in the past, it remains within the European (post-)colonial paradigm of a country that wants to share its culture and knowledge with the world, without sufficient interest in taking a closer look at how and what it could learn constitutionally from other countries outside Europe, especially the Global South. As this paper has illustrated, however, there is much to be learned from other constitutions, especially from the Global South and particularly for Austria.

Based on a knowledge-based perspective on comparative constitutional studies, the opening up of comparative constitutional law to a truly global agenda must include the Global South. The engagement in such a comparative agenda needs to be open to a pluralistic world of constitutional law and constitutional culture, which goes far beyond traditional European understandings of constitutional law.

Colliding '*Regards-Croisés*' and Autochthonous Constitutional *Ethos*

Comparative Constitutional Law from Pluralism to Introspection

Pablo Riberi

esse est percipi
Berkeley (Principles: 3)

A. Introduction

Comparative constitutional law is a rewarding source of inspiration for constitutional drafters, lawmakers, judges, officeholders, legal operators, scholars, and individuals in general. It can be a fundamental tool for grappling with puzzling rights adjudication or the breakdown of polity powers. Indeed, it deserves our attention as it provides sound and practical knowledge. Under this scope, *ex hypothesis*, I would like to frame the '*regards croisés*' debate on the specific alternative when opposing Global North and Global South stances may interplay under strain.

Comparative constitutional analysis requires sorting out relevant data within a commonly accepted technical discourse. This statement drives concrete methodological challenges for those seeking a comprehensive collective understanding of constitutional phenomena. My insight is that, through '*regards croisés*', such methodological challenges bestow a basic certitude: Diverse perspectives entail diverse perceptions. Naturally, it is impossible to find a neutral 'panopticon', let alone to raise one's sight from two different standpoints. So, acknowledging that diverse approaches may bring about conflicting perceptions, the question is how an impartial observer can develop a reliable comparative discourse in constitutional law.

My understanding of the issue relies on two conceptual insights: one philosophically crafted by Hannah Arendt and the other by Charles Taylor. The former grapples with autochthonous thinking, and the latter deals with identity as a baseline for authenticity.

According to the records of a conference honoring the "Work of Hannah Arendt", held at the University of Toronto in November 1972, Arendt coined the following metaphor in the German language: Denken ohne Geländer ("thinking without a banister").[1] She pushed forward this statement during a conversation with prominent scholars. What Arendt wanted to underscore with this idea is that relying on one's experience of thinking in isolation can be randomly rewarding. It requires withdrawing oneself from thinking with others.

Charles Taylor's concept of identity acknowledges the need for otherness; it requires pushing forward one's confronting identity toward those belonging to others.[2] Besides, there is no existing being unless there is a plural recognition of its uniqueness. From several scholarly, prestigious Global North centers, Global South constitutional problems, challenges, and responses have deserved little or no attention. When they do, the Global North's assessments usually fall short or oversimplify the importance or value of others' outlooks. Taking notice of such misrepresentation, as well as the complexity of the social, economic, and political hurdles in different settings, autochthonous constitutional development looks overriding for securing the rule of law and a thriving democracy.[3]

From a deep Global South perspective, this text aims to achieve two primary goals. On the one hand, by reflecting on the overwhelming influence of Global North normative viewpoints, I will argue in favor of the Global South's reluctance to blindly follow hegemonic *prêt-à-porter* normative responses and solutions imported from the former.[4] On the other hand, harnessing two concrete historical situations, I will portray how Global North's prestigious insights may undermine or dismantle autochthonous constitutional developments entrenched within the Global South constitutional *ethos*.[5]

---

[1] Arendt borrows the idea from the Greek historian Stan Draenos. See *Arendt, Hannah*, "Hannah Arendt on Hannah Arendt", in Thinking without a Banister -Essays in Understanding 1953–1975, Schocken Books, 2018, p. 473.

[2] Charles Taylor writes that "the acknowledgment of our identity requires the recognition by others". See *Taylor, Charles*, The Ethics of Authenticity, Harvard University Press, 1991, p. 45.

[3] Concerning populist development, Mark Tushnet grapples with the idea of distinctive legal, cultural, and autochthonous constitutional interpretation. See *Tushnet, Mark*, "Can there be autochthonous methods of constitutional interpretation", in Gardós-Orosz, Fruzsina and Szente, Zoltán (eds.), Populist Challenges to Constitutional Interpretation in Europe and Beyond, Routledge, 2021, p. 71.

[4] Although I resort to the plain meaning of the word "hegemony", it would be worthwhile to visit deeper layers of its philosophical usage. For example, from the Stoics or Machiavelli and other Marxist thinkers, the word hegemony – 'Το ηγεμονικον' – implies the existence of a distinctive quality of something that, once generalized, reveals a factual sense of superiority and preeminence. According to Gramsci, a primary reference in its political utterance is that hegemony implies the presence of an actual or threatening force and the probability of consolidating a dominant consensus over the unbalanced power situation in civil society. Hegemonic power hovers over institutions and all cultural environments. See *Gramsci, Antonio*, La Política y el Estado Moderno, Planeta Agostini, 1993.

[5] For a deeper grasp of what the word *ethos* means, see *Bubner, Rüdiger*, Acción, Historia y Orden Institucional, Fondo de Cultura Económica, 2009, pp. 197–201.

If there is a double-track way of constitutional observations, the likelihood of opposing standpoints becomes an empirical certitude. Naturally, the rejection or consolidation of the Global North's constitutional influence in Latin America has heavily depended on philosophical, theoretical, and practical legacies embedded in a common historical bedrock. Besides, these endowments reflect shared civilized expectations. Be that as it may, by presenting opposing stances, I will showcase how dominant normative standards or adjudicatory criteria imported from the Global North are sometimes detrimental or inadequate for the Global South's concrete constitutional challenges. I will delve into the patronizing mindset that validates these undetected influences in Latin America. Naturally, I am not aiming at any concrete legacy that has enriched Latin American legal culture.

Besides, there is a well-entrenched history of constitutional accomplishment in Latin America.[6] Although Global North works acknowledging Latin American contributions are scarce, I am not interested in analyzing any cultural colonialism whatsoever.[7] My take is more essential. At least from a Latin American standpoint, I want to champion a kind of reasonable constitutional suspicion when these '*regards croisés*' fall under strain or disagree. This deserves utmost attention from a Latin American perspective, as the perception, acceptance, or rejection of the Global North's constitutional influence appears cumbersome.

In more abstract terms, Global South scholars and ordinary people should feel thankful for a wide range of philosophical, political, and institutional legacies endowed by Western colonial nations.[8] I feel at ease endorsing this sentiment. All things considered, however, it is also interesting to recall that some legacies and gifts are worthy of second-guessing. The Trojans learned this lesson too late. They belatedly understood that the concealed goal of the wooden horse was not to honor but to conquer them.

In short, I will funnel my way through five stages. Firstly, I will introduce my concerns and essential insights. Secondly, I will frame the scope of my contribution. I will elaborate on a basic caveat and other methodological insights during the third phase. Afterward, in the following stage, I will focus my analysis on two historical constitutional developments where the Global South's and Global North's '*regards croisés*' collided. Finally, I will share the concluding remarks.

---

[6] See *Gargarella, Roberto*, Latin American Constitutionalism 1810–2010 -The Engine Room of the Constitution-, Oxford University Press, 2023, pp. 62–84.

[7] I celebrate Prof. Dann's "Southern Turn" and his openness toward the TWAIL – Third World approach to International Law. See *Dann, Philipp*, "Southern Turn, Northern Implications: rethinking the meaning of colonial legacies for Colonial Comparative Constitutional Studies", in Comparative Constitutional Studies (Vol. 1, No. 2, June 2023), pp. 174–180.

[8] According to Norbert Elias, civilizing and decivilizing processes exist. It is interesting how Elias provides an analytical distinction between civilization and culture. See *Elias, Norbert*, El Proceso de la Civilización, Fondo de Cultura Económica, 2012, pp. 83–90.

B. Framing the Issue and Main Insights

This text aims for two goals: Firstly, to advance practical considerations about Latin American epistemic capacity to articulate the value of comparative constitutional law lessons. From a Latin American independent perspective, such determination implies enhancing the self-mastering of legal, political, cultural, and moral pathways leading to unraveling either the admission or rejection of Global North's influence. From a Latin American viewpoint, this critical capacity presupposes the existence of diverse kinds of global conversations. Most of them resemble top-down monologues, whereas others look like dialogues between parties on an equal footing.[9]

Secondly, I will present two concrete historical developments to provide a comprehensive dimension of the direct and indirect detrimental effects of the Global North's hegemonic influence on legitimizing a stringent set of constitutional responses. The consolidation of the Global North's influence has heavily depended on deeply rooted standards and normative criteria embedded in its cultural prestige. Such circumstances have somehow shaped civilized expectations around the world. In this sense, by presenting opposing stances, I will showcase how autochthonous democratic and constitutional solutions in countries like Argentina have been foiled by a thick barrier of theoretical bias imported from the Global North's dominant mindset.

I would also like to note that, regardless of how sophisticated and valuable the pre-Columbian cultures may have been – I am referring fundamentally to those developed in South America – there is no pre-Columbian constitutional discipline as such, nor is it possible to find alternative theoretical or conceptual elements of study where neither Power nor Freedom has ever been a theoretical subject. Nevertheless, there is, of course, knowledge in these local experiences; for example, concerning the normative status of 'Nature' and the way native communities perceived themselves as an indivisible collective being peacefully dwelling in Nature's womb.[10]

Finally, another insight can be portrayed as follows. When concrete benefits outweigh this principled stance, intelligent cultural resilience toward the Global

---

[9] Dann defends the search for new themes and the need to broaden Global North's comparative scope. See *Dann, Philipp*, "Southern Turn, Northern Implications: rethinking the meaning of colonial legacies for colonial comparative constitutional studies", in Comparative Constitutional Studies (Vol. 1, No. 2, June 2023), p. 188.

[10] The Argentine Constitution, for example, acknowledges the ethnic and cultural pre-existence of the Indigenous peoples of Argentina. Article 75; § 17 CA provides: "to guarantee respect for the identity and the right to bilingual and intercultural education; to recognize the legal capacity of their communities, and the community possession and ownership of the lands they traditionally occupy; and to regulate the granting of other lands adequate for human development; none of them shall be sold, transmitted or subject to liens or attachments. To guarantee their participation in issues related to their natural resources and other interests affecting them. The provinces may jointly exercise these powers".

North's normative and institutional developments may be forsaken. Resilience is justifiable only if such rejection is an intelligent one. Besides, it is also worth noting Philipp Dann's extensive contribution to the subject by proposing a methodological upheaval in comparative constitutional law. Through what he calls 'slow comparison', Dann takes notice of singular constitutional experiences drawn from the Global South.[11] Likewise, I also endorse Konrad Lachmayer's persistent yearning for more pluralism in the field.[12]

C. Methodological Caveat

I. General Insights

I start with three preliminary questions.

1. Can we avoid grappling with epistemological and methodological questions? – My answer is: not at all. The observer must simultaneously engage with epistemological and methodological questions.

2. Should diverse constitutional perspectives reflect together the very same description of a single constitutional phenomenon? – My answer to this question is dubious. It depends on what kind of phenomenon we are dealing with.

3. Is it sensible to discredit one perspective's account because such perception may overlook undetected traits from the other angle? – Here, my answer is yes. Regarding constitutional issues, the Global South's outweighing authority may result from experiencing such enduring problems and challenges.

The perception of any phenomenon implies a level of 'awareness' from the subject. Each perception entails a state of self-consciousness connecting the perceiving subject and the perceived object.[13] From a Latin American comparative perspective, it is impossible to have reliable knowledge of its constitutional phenomena – e.g., over institutions, materials, and proceedings – unless such perceptions reflect a nuanced concert of Global South's constitutional values, beliefs, and interests.[14]

---

[11] Specifically addressing the effects of colonialism on the North-South/South-North link, in line with what he calls "methodological pluralism", Dann also favors a functionalist contextualist approach to CCS. See *Dann, Philipp*, "Southern Turn, Northern Implications: rethinking the meaning of colonial legacies for colonial comparative constitutional studies", in Comparative Constitutional Studies (Vol. 1, No. 2, June 2023), pp. 174–180.

[12] Konrad Lachmayer in an exciting text, lays down the theoretical framework for bringing pluralism to comparative constitutional law. See *Lachmayer, Konrad*, "The Possibility of International Constitutional Law: A pluralistic Approach Towards Constitutional Law", in Riberi, Pablo and Lachmayer, Konrad (eds.), Philosophical or Political Foundation of Constitutional Law? -Perspectives in Conflict-, Nomos-Facultas, 2014, pp. 289–311.

[13] See *Berger, Peter and Luckmann, Thomas*, Modernidad, Pluralismo y Crisis de Sentido, Ediciones Paidós, 1997, pp. 79–125.

[14] Charles Taylor underscores that "discovering my identity doesn't mean that I work it

The Global North's hegemonic approach in comparative constitutional law reminds me of Carlos Astrada's broader criticism of Alexander Kojève's philosophy of history. Based on a dialectic reading of individual and collective freedom, the former had prematurely dawned on unattended economic and social hazards that the 'end of history decree' proclaimed by Kojève – and later by Fukuyama – might have brought about to other nations of the Global South. More than half a century ago, Astrada also reacted against a polyphemic way of addressing history. From a Southern perspective, when historical events were simultaneously developing in various parts of the planet, the end of history, as the Northern-developed capitalist countries might have envisioned, looks like a *non-sequitur* worldwide conclusion.[15]

For several reasons, the '*regards croisés*' do not meet halfway.[16] Whatever the distance, my concern is to isolate the importance of Southern self-reliant assessment of their constitutional issues. It is also rewarding to acknowledge that a broader and deeper understanding of constitutional matters requires recognizing different angles. In this vein, Prof. Dann stresses the importance of studying the constitutional experiences drawn from the Global South. As stated before, he promotes 'slow comparison' while engaging with what he calls the 'Southern Turn'.[17]

Regarding the statement of the epigraph: 'esse est percipi', the reference aims to highlight how the constitutional corpus subject to comparison heavily depends on the observer's capacity to reach out to unfamiliar foreign materials. There can be no record of original constitutional problems, nor is it possible to have an account of alternative normative solutions unless the comparativist observer cautiously engages in unveiling the multilayered constitutional phenomena. Furthermore, from a Latin American standpoint, it implies the observer's capacity to connect the dots from unfamiliar problems to subsequent constitutional

out in isolation but that I negotiate it through dialogue, partly overt, partly internalized, with others. That is why the development of an ideal of inwardly generated identity gives a crucial importance to recognition. My own identity crucially depends on my dialogical relations with others". See *Taylor, Charles*, The Ethics of Authenticity, Harvard University Press, 1991, pp. 47–48.

[15] See *Astrada, Carlos*, Dialéctica e Historia -Hegel y Marx-, Juarez Editor, 1969, pp. 95–98.

[16] It is impossible to determine where the Global South and the Global North opposing normative outlooks encounter. There are counterfactuals and countless hypotheses to deal with. As far as this text is concerned, it is pointless to explore what would have happened if, during the 15th century, Montezuma had landed in Gibraltar or Normandy? In 'Guns, Steel & Germs', under the chapter title 'Collision in Cajamarca', Jared Diamond wonders 'why the Inca Atahualpa did not capture King Charles I of Spain'. See *Diamond, Jared*, Guns, Steel & Germs, WW Norton & Company, 1999, pp. 67–81.

[17] See *Dann, Philipp*, "Southern Turn, Northern Implications: rethinking the meaning of colonial legacies for colonial comparative constitutional studies", in Comparative Constitutional Studies (Vol. 1, No. 2, June 2023), pp. 192–193.

responses. Far beyond a simple scholarly discrepancy, history reveals that when the Global South's outlook conveys different assessments of diagnoses or remedies, such discrepancies can bring about devastating consequences.

Comparative lessons are more fertile when challenging constitutional situations are plurally portrayed 'in situ'. Indeed, when many engaged minds can delve deep into all the complexities at stake or when the comparativist experts can thoroughly examine the legal materials, institutions, or procedures under investigation.[18] Having said this, I propose concentrating on three essential questions:

1. Why is it important to study comparative law by resorting to plural perspectives?
2. What constitutional observations can be valuable from both the Global North's and Global South's standpoints?
3. In what way may South-North cross-cutting perspectives enhance comparative knowledge in constitutional law?

II. Five Basic Ideas

Exploring the nuts and bolts of my methodological concerns, let me start by highlighting a basic intuition that I can synthesize in the following terms: "Observation is loaded with theory".[19] When grappling with foreign constitutional materials – as may also happen with almost every scientific collection of samples and data – a key caveat requires setting up some ancillary epistemic safeguards. Any comparativist or constitutional expert must never underestimate the unfathomed layers of misunderstandings looming from a shallow account of any unfamiliar object under inspection. The rhetoric of constitutional law may appear similar on the surface, though seldom is it so in-depth.[20]

In short, I will summarize five of my main methodological concerns.[21]

1. In comparative constitutional law, framing the epistemic latitude of each '*regard croisé*' requires grappling with a two-pronged set of basic questions. It

[18] See *Lachmayer, Konrad*, "The Possibility of International Constitutional Law: A pluralistic Approach Towards Constitutional Law", in Riberi, Pablo and Lachmayer, Konrad (eds.), Philosophical or Political Foundation of Constitutional Law? -Perspectives in Conflict-, Nomos-Facultas, 2014, pp. 308–309.

[19] See *Hanson, Norwood R.*, Patrones de descubrimiento: investigación de las bases conceptuales de la Ciencia, Alianza, 1985.

[20] Regarding constitutional failures, Elkins, Ginsburg and Melton provide factual examples where contrasting outcomes come from similar contexts. See *Elkins, Zachery, Ginsburg, Tom and Melton, James*, The Endurance of the Constitution, Cambridge University Press, 2010, pp. 147–178.

[21] Regarding methodology, the following bibliography provided by Global North scholars is worth noticing. For example, *Tushnet, Mark*, Advanced Introduction to Comparative Constitutional Law, Edward & Elgar Publishing, 2014. Likewise, *Jackson, Vicky and Tushnet, Mark*, Comparative Constitutional Law, Thompson West, 2006. Also, *Rosenfeld, Michel and Sajó, András* (eds.), The Oxford Handbook of Comparative Constitutional Law, Oxford University Press, 2013. Also, *Kischel, Uwe*, Comparative Law, Oxford University Press, 2019.

requires spelling out 'what we see' and 'how we see' because observation is loaded with theory. In other words, well-entrenched biases and subtle experiences are unconsciously modeling the perception of the external world.[22] To put it simply, as I have underscored above, the thesis of 'theory-laden observations', defended by Hanson, operates as the most significant linchpin of my methodological concerns.[23]

2. For practical reasons, using English as a *lingua franca* seems sensible. It is, however, necessary to know that some meaningful language nuances involved in the Latin American constitutional discourse are hardly noticed by any mechanical translation from Spanish – or Portuguese – into English.[24] The purported concept or idea conveyed in constitutional writing materials and utterances is likely to be couched by a concert of concrete reasons, goals, and emotions that have been reshaping its meaning.

3. Comparative constitutional law can be much more rewarding if its contributions enhance a multidisciplinary approach for *lege-lata* analysis and *lege-ferenda* proposals. In both situations, the assessment of comparative constitutional law is likely to display superficial similarities and differences among the inspected orders.[25]

When engaged in comparison, the observer must discern how facts and norms are usually under strain. To avoid the 'naturalistic fallacy', the comparativist

[22] Here, it resonates with Nietzsche's claim: "How the True World has become a fable; the History of an Error". See *Nietzsche, Friedrich*, Verdad y Mentira, Editorial miluno, p. 129.

[23] According to Hanson and the so-called theory-laden, "perceiving" or "seeing" usually involves a process of conscious visual experience conducted by the observer with the object under his scientific observation. However, Hanson's theory-ladenness explores the extent to which a foundation of cognitive psychology determines how we see/perceive and what we see/perceive. In other words, how sensory information conforms to the underlying, dominant theory about information. Based on a previous stage in which there is observational data, the interplay of memory and communications shapes the situation's understanding. See *Hanson, Norwood R.*, Patrones de descubrimiento: investigación de las bases conceptuales de la Ciencia, Alianza, 1985. Also, *Khun, Thomas S.*, ¿Qué son las revoluciones Científicas?, Altaya, 1995, pp. 95–151.

[24] Mark Tushnet has also dealt with this issue. See *Tushnet, Mark*, "Can there be autonomous methods of constitutional interpretation?", in Gardós-Orosz, Fruzsina and Szente, Zoltán (eds.), Populist Challenges to Constitutional Interpretation in Europe and Beyond, Routledge, 2021, p. 64.

[25] The fact is that similar constitutional texts and practices are likely to develop into divergent interpretations. That is to say, the academic view or that of the legislator, judge, or interpreter in general follows winding paths. Sometimes, similar normative meanings come from different legal provisions and/or constitutional settings. This happens even when the constitutional materials or practices do not belong to assimilable design, tradition, or history. On the contrary, the interpretation may set itself free from the original canon even with analogous contexts, hastening a distorted or even contradictory semantic scope. See *Riberi, Pablo*, "La Forma Constitucional -Especulaciones sobre la Apariencia de un Ente sin Contornos-", in Riberi, Pablo and Salazar, Pedro (eds.), Forma Constitucional y Decisión Democrática, Ediciones del Instituto de Investigaciones Jurídicas UNAM, 2022, pp. 36–42.

must sort out explanatory reasons from justifying reasons.[26] The former conveys descriptive statements, whereas the latter involves normative ones. This is necessary when grappling with relevant facts entwined with complex legal assessments.

4. Acknowledging how legal/philosophical constitutionalism and political constitutionalism enable different types of legitimizing narratives allows the comparativist observer to avoid semantic and pragmatic misunderstandings.[27] For example, regarding the consolidated inclination to resort to legal transplants and case-law borrowings, such wariness allows the comparativist observer to discover the Global North's hegemonic influence in Latin American courts.[28]

Concerning constitutional design, before criticizing failures or praising successful reforms, the comparativist observer must be suspicious and pay maximum attention to all causation links involved in his observations.[29] The lessons extracted from ongoing observations of institutional and political reforms are very illuminating. They teach us how vital prudence is when assessing unforeseen consequences and potential secondary effects. Besides, the replication and adaptation of Global North's successful constitutional experiences have seldom operated by the original template.[30]

5. Taking advantage of the comparative tools provided by contextualism while adapting them for the sake of a 'structuralist' understanding provides the comparativist observer with a more expansive range of valuable knowledge. Although my understanding of contextualism aligns with Uwe Kischel's standpoint, the structural scope allows digging deeper and reaching new layers of constitutional depth.[31] By ferreting around timely and concrete political, socio-

[26] Hume addressed the '*is-ought*' issue in his "Treatise of Human Nature" – first published in 1739–1740 – while George E. Moore does it *On the Naturalistic Fallacy* at the Proceedings of the British Academy Volume L, Lectures and Memoirs (1964). From a metaethical standpoint, Hume and Moore criticize other philosophers for deriving propositions expressing obligations from factual premises. Also see *Fate Norton, David* (ed.), The Cambridge Companion to Hume, Cambridge University Press, 1999, pp. 168–169. Additionally, Frankena's contributions to the subject are worth noticing. See *Frankena, William K.*, "The Naturalistic Fallacy", in Cahn, Steven M. and Haber, Joram G. (eds.), 20th Century Ethical Theory, Prentice Hall, 1995, pp. 129–138.

[27] *Riberi, Pablo*, "An Uncertain Dilemma: Philosophical or Political Foundation for Constitutional Law", in Riberi, Pablo and Lachmayer, Konrad (eds.), Philosophical or Political Foundation of Constitutional Law -Perspectives in Conflict-, Nomos-Facultas, 2014, pp. 33–75.

[28] See *Riberi, Pablo*, "A Constitutional Caveat: How much Legitimate Meaning Comes Along Implementing Legal Transplants?", in Rivista di Diritto Pubblico Comparato ed Europeo, Fascicolo 1 Anno 2013, pp. 101–111.

[29] See *Elster, Jon*, "Clearing and Strengthening the Channels of Constitutional Making", in Ginsburg, Tom (ed.), Comparative Constitutional Design, Cambridge University Press, 2013, pp. 15–31.

[30] Russell Hardin analyzes trust management and how this fundamental emotion may thrive in institutional bodies and civil society. *Hardin, Russell*, Trust & Trustworthiness, Russell Sage Foundation, 2002, pp. 133–151.

[31] In this regard, Professor Uwe Kischel's contribution deserves attention. For the sake of

logical, and/or economic traits, the observer can explore new meaningful edges and profiles portraying an ever-changing constitutional setting.[32]

Let me elaborate on this idea. Nobody can understand what a finger is unless he has learned in advance what a hand is. The comparativist observer, perhaps, can be clueless or have a shallow idea of how judicial review works in a country like Venezuela. In this sense, for example, my claim is that everybody is doomed to ignorance unless he adopts a broader outlook encompassing the Global South's history of hyper-presidentialism and populism.

D. Analysis: How much attention do foreign law and scholars' opinions deserve?

Global North's philosophical, theoretical, and practical lessons have enlightened and inspired Latin American constitutional developments. Since the early 19th century, the emancipated Latin American nations have copied the constitutional experiences of the United States and France. Migrating political ideas have sedimented in countless institutional settings. Therefore, Global South and Global North '*regards croisés*' not only look attractive but are also unavoidable for understanding the makings of nuanced constitutional orders. Moreover, Global North's constitutional ideas and experiments operate as a guiding roadmap for Latin American constitutional design.[33]

Consequently, when the viewpoints of prestigious Global North experts collide with those of the Global South, the latter undergoes a significant political, legal, and economic impact. Whatever the reasons and results, engaging in foreign insights and legal borrowing has become a critical dimension for comparative constitutional law in both hemispheres.[34] My concern, however, is to prevent the mechanical imposition of Global South domestic values, principles, and

strictly doctrinal analysis, through traditional methodologies, this author sharply explores common grounds among compared legal systems. See *Kischel, Uwe*, Comparative Law, Oxford University Press, 2019, pp. 87–102.

[32] Structuralist approaches have developed in different fields of knowledge, from linguistics (Saussure) to sociology (Durkheim) or anthropology (Lévi-Strauss). They encompass far-reaching epistemic and methodological fields aiming to unravel broader and deeper cultural patterns that surround all that human beings can do, think, perceive, and feel.

[33] There are important Global North theoretical influences. For example, after wondering how universal comparative constitutional law is, Ran Hirschl explores what allegedly are supposed to be common grounds for a universalist approach. See *Hirschl, Ran*, Comparative Matters, Oxford University Press, 2016, pp. 192–200.

[34] For example, the operation of borrowing implies an "analogical reasoning" which, in terms of Jefferson White's approach, means a general "normative interpretation" according to which the factual similarity between an undecided (local) case and a (foreign) case, both situations are tackled as if they were the same. See *White, Jefferson*, "Analogical Reasoning", in Patterson, Dennis (ed.), A Companion to Philosophy of Law and Legal Theory, Blackwell Publishers, 2001, pp. 583–589.

rules, let alone a voluntary subordination of Global South's autochthonous constitutional ethos. Let me elaborate on this.

For example, the hegemonic influence of the Global North may drive Southern scholars, legislators, and judges to adjust their political, constitutional, and/or institutional responses to a limited array of imported solutions extracted from the Global North's past experiences when not purposefully tailored by their books and lectures. By accommodating the narrative of the given circumstances to the Global North's theoretical framing, vocabulary/semantics, and value considerations, the hegemonic stance impairs the natural development of the constitutional *ethos* in place. Such influence has been detrimental to a self-reliant constitutional engagement in Latin America.[35]

For a more comprehensive understanding of the constitutional backdrop in Latin America, it is crucial to broaden the comparative lenses and also to deepen its focus inwardly. Having an account of the underlying historical circumstances enables a sound contextualist approach as well as a comprehensive structural understanding of situated constitutional developments.[36] Reflecting on the reciprocal interplay of the social and economic orders allows the observer to provide a thorough assessment of how supervening legal order stabilizes both realms. Naturally, all these elements perform dialectically in their transformative dynamic. The slightest change in any of them brings about a subsequent alteration in the other. By adapting its rules, principles, and values, the legal order reflects such alterations.[37]

Now, let me underline something important. The implied criticism conveyed by the following cases is in no way downplaying Global North's enlightening influence, nor does it disregard its civilizational legacy.[38] From a theoretical and doctrinal point of view, for example, both Orentlicher's and Armin von Bogdandy's sound opinions deserve the utmost attention.[39] Strictly speaking, the problem is a practical one. If there is any responsibility, it should be borne by local operators who recklessly resort to foreign doctrinal sources of legitimacy. In what sense is this conduct reprehensible? In the sense that, by following the savvy dictates of Global North's legislators, judges, and scholars, the Global South's autochthonous development of constitutional culture is increasingly in jeopardy.

[35] See *Astrada, Carlos*, Dialéctica e Historia -Hegel y Marx-, Juarez Editor, 1969, pp. 45–59.

[36] This is particularly meaningful when analyzing Latin American polities' processes of constitutional change. For a better grasp, see *Negretto, Gabriel*, La Política del Cambio Constitucional en América Latina, Fondo de Cultura Económica, 2015, pp. 66–104.

[37] During the 2024 conference organized by the German Society of Comparative Law at the Humboldt University in Berlin, Prathama Banerjee championed a more radical stand challenging Global North hegemonic influences.

[38] See *Bloom, Philip*, Encyclopédie, Anagrama, 2007, pp. 126–127.

[39] See *von Bogdandy, Armin*, Por un Derecho Común para América Latina, Siglo XXI Editores, 2020, pp. 31–99; also see *Orentlicher, Diane*, "Settling Accounts: The Duty to Prosecute Human Rights Violations of a Prior Regime", 100 Yale Law Journal (1991).

Before presenting these two concrete cases where the '*regards croisés*' conveyed conflicting views, let me share information concerning the political mindset and the historical backdrop of Argentina's constitutional conundrums.

I. Historical and Intellectual Background in Argentina

1. Alberdi, Sarmiento, and Foreign Law

Juan Bautista Alberdi was one of the forefathers of Argentine state-building during the 19th century. He designed the main guidelines for political institutions while envisioning modern Argentina in the 20th century. After studying and comparing national and subnational constitutions, especially the American Constitution of 1787 and the Chilean Constitution of 1833, he managed to draft a politically successful blueprint for the Argentine Constitution.

To better understand the makings of the Argentine Constitution, the observer must take notice of the interplay of autochthonous insights with foreign influences. From a historical perspective, the drafters had two preferred sources of inspiration: on the one hand, Alberdi's constitutional blueprint, "Bases y Puntos de Partida para la Organización Nacional"[40]; on the other, the Constitution of the USA.[41]

Alberdi did not hesitate to explore other continental experiences and borrow constitutional responses from different countries. He outlined the possible Argentina of his time from the perspective of an enlightened elite, of which he was one of the most notable members.

In short, Alberdi compared U.S. subnational state law with other constitutional experiments of the Americas. Based on these comparative insights, he produced a comprehensive proposal. Deeply involved in current political discussions, Alberdi, an incredibly talented man, is to Argentina what Madison is to the U.S. constitutional history.

In his view, the Constitution should serve as a new public framework for education, immigration, liberty, and social development. The new republic should promote reasonable and negotiated by-products for the sake of political stability. His work was successful: It resulted in a practical constitution providing a new order that became a steppingstone for a time of progress marked by economic growth and cultural modernization.[42]

---

[40] See *Alberdi, Juan B.*, Bases y Puntos de Partida para la Organización Nacional, Editorial Plus Ultra, 1981.

[41] See *García Mansilla, Manuel and Ramírez Calvo, Ricardo*, La Constitución Nacional y la Obsesión Antinorteamericana, Editorial Virtudes, 2008.

[42] I have analyzed how discrete doses of dissent, distrust, and pessimism will likely bring benign constitutional effects in Latin America. See *Riberi, Pablo*, "Disenso, Pesimismo y Desconfianza dentro de los Límites de las Normas Constitucionales", in Bergman, Marcelo and Rosenkrantz, Carlos (eds.), Confianza y Derecho en América Latina, Fondo de Cultura Económica-CIDE, 2009, pp. 195–216.

In his approach, Alberdi understood the close link between collective preferences, private interests, and individual rights. He did this when the country was at the very beginning of its constitutional life. This is why he thought about other times and other people who were about to come to Argentina. Through feasible means, he dared to design incentives to attract hard-working European immigrants to the country.[43] Alberdi's primary concern was to seed a fertile constitutional environment for future generations of Argentineans.

Alberdi's key constitutional goals were immigration and education. These objectives hastened constitutional policies that were supposed to be fundamental for the young, ignorant, and underpopulated nation. Alberdi's aims were evident as he laid down an order of rights within a republican constitutional framework geared toward the European model of civilization. Following the Enlightenment legacy, he believed reason could change the country's dire fate. Nevertheless, he knew that only time could transform people's preferences, which were in disarray and facing violent conflicts. He acted according to the circumstances, but his thinking was projective. He relied on the liberal philosophy of the time, whether adapted to the local mindset.

It is indisputable that Sarmiento, a public figure, and former President, wanted Argentine courts to follow case law precedents of the U.S. Supreme Court (USSC). There was a clear distinction between those who championed rational normativism as the underlying theoretical foundation of the Constitution – like Sarmiento – and those, like Alberdi, who were willing to instill a twist of legal historicism into those liberal insights. The harsh epistolary debate between these two towering intellectuals provides a flavor of such clashing perspectives during the 19th century. While Alberdi selectively cherished institutional and legal practices ingrained in the Spanish tradition, Sarmiento rejected all of them.

Alberdi wanted the Argentine legal identity to reflect the spirit of the law. He believed this identity (and spiritedness) should be rooted in concrete experience, whereas Sarmiento insisted on shaping the Argentine legal system according to the U.S. template. Furthermore, Sarmiento even envisioned the authoritative enforcement of USSC case law in Argentine domestic trials.[44] Alberdi's thinking was that of a savvy scholar; Sarmiento was a well-educated politician. Herder, Guizot, Savigny, Lemminier, and Jouffroy heavily influenced Alberdi's ideas.[45] Both were engaged in transforming the social and economic matrix of the nation.

---

[43] Article 25 of the Argentine Constitution provides (that): The Federal Government shall foster European immigration; and may not restrict, limit or burden with any tax whatsoever the entry into the Argentine territory of foreigners who arrive to till the soil, improve industries, and introducing and teaching arts, and sciences.

[44] See *Rosenkrantz, Carlos*, "Against Borrowing and Other Nonauthoritative uses of Foreign Law", International Journal of Constitutional Law (Vol. 1, No. 2, April 2003), p. 288.

[45] *Ghirardi, Olsen*, La Filosofia en Alberdi, Ediciones de la Academia Nacional de Derecho de Córdoba, 1993, pp. 11–32.

2. The Argentine Constitutional Setting

As stressed above, there was an extended period of civil wars following the Argentine Revolution. Although subject to fierce negotiation, the Argentine Constitution became a successful one. Inspired by the U.S. Constitution and modeled by Alberdi's pragmatic blueprint, it exemplifies what Roberto Gargarella calls "fusion constitutionalism". In other words, conservative and liberal political stances compromised their tenets for the sake of enacting the fundamental law.[46]

Benjamin Gorostiaga, a founding father of the Constitution, stated that the Argentine Constitution was "cast in the mold of the Constitution of the United States". Accordingly, bicameralism, federalism, and a clear separation of powers – all distinctive traits of the U.S. document – are also visible in the Argentine Constitution. The Argentine Constitution provided a bill of rights in the first part of the document, which mirrors the U.S. Bill of Rights and the French Declaration of the Rights of Man and the Citizen.[47]

Despite this promising outset, the political branches have seldom been able to achieve and secure the aims enshrined in the preamble. There is a dramatic departure from the U.S. model regarding the interplay of the state branches. Today, the Argentine presidential system has wholly drifted away from the original U.S. separation of powers model.[48] The Argentine polity operates as a system of presidential preeminence, imperial presidentialism, or has straightforwardly become hyper-presidentialist. In terms of constitutional *ethos*, Argentina has an unbalanced copy of its original template.[49]

---

[46] What is 'fusion' constitutionalism? Gargarella has stressed its most fundamental traits. The early successful constitutionalism in Latin America was a mixture of liberal and conservative compromises that came along to provide order and state authority. Besides, both stances favored a unitary form of State, and they mistrusted local governments. For example, the Argentine Constitution of 1853, Mexico in 1857, Peru in 1860, Paraguay in 1870, and Brazil in 1891. Following the author's insights, these features are helpful to grasp this concept better: 1. Religious tolerance and state neutrality, though the Catholic church had some privileges, 2. Checks and Balances; yet with strong executives, 3. Neither federalism nor unitary territorial organization, 4. Individualistic liberal rights were granted; political rights and civic participation were undermined. See *Gargarella, Roberto*, Latin American Constitutionalism 1810–2010 -The Engine Room of the Constitution-, Oxford University Press, 2023.

[47] The U.S. "*Bill of Rights*" (the first ten amendments) was enacted on December 15, 1791, and the "*Déclaration des droits de l'Homme et du Citoyen*" on August 26, 1789.

[48] It is interesting to notice how political constitutionalism has developed different understandings of the separation of powers. Alexander Somek elaborates on this idea. See *Somek, Alexander*, Cosmopolitan Constitution, Oxford University Press, 2014, pp. 56–58.

[49] Concerning constitutional design, term limits, and political crisis, Ginsburg, Elkins, and Melton provide a sound descriptive analysis. See *Ginsburg, Tom, Elkins, Zachary and Melton, James*, "Do Executive Term Limits Cause Constitutional Crisis?", in Ginsburg, Tom (ed.), Comparative Constitutional Design, Cambridge University Press, 2013, pp. 351–381.

3. Selective Borrowing and Legal Transplants

As stated, in countries of the region, there is a consolidated interpretative trend in which legislators, judges, and scholars usually resort to foreign law.[50] Additionally, there is another layer of constitutional constructions that have drifted away from the original templates; political and legal drafters and interpreters are developing their responses to common constitutional problems. In any case, from a comparative perspective, both trends deserve the utmost attention.

It is interesting to trace back case law records to better depict how the U.S. constitutional model influenced Argentine courts. From the very outset of the republic, the Argentine Supreme Court (SCJN) made extraordinary efforts to follow the U.S. Supreme Court's doctrine concerning judicial review and quote USSC jurisprudence in rights adjudication. Consequently, the Argentine SCJN and other lower courts have always been steadfast in borrowing from USSC constitutional constructions.[51] Let me mention a couple of examples to illustrate this situation.

In 1887, in the case of "Sojo", the SCJN struck down Section 20 of the 1848 Act, which granted original jurisdiction to the Court on habeas corpus cases.[52] Citing U.S. case law, in line with Marshall in "Marbury", the Argentine highest court reasoned that the Constitution prevented any statutory expansion of the State branches' powers. Later, other decisions related to welfare policies, or "social constitutionalism", also sought inspiration from U.S. case law. For example, "Ercolano"[53], and "Avico v. De la Pesa"[54], concerning lowering interest rates and a moratorium on the foreclosure of existing mortgage contracts, were cases where the Argentine Highest Court duplicated the USSC Court criteria.[55] Particularly, to bring tokens of the "Great Society and Welfare State paradigm", the Argentine Supreme Court was heavily influenced by cases like "Home-building"[56] and "Nebbia".[57]

As I noted in a previous text, comparative constitutional law may provide a supplementary source of normative reasons. They may also enlarge the domestic

[50] Ramírez Calvo and García-Mansilla wrote a thorough analysis of U.S. constitutional influence in Argentina. See *García-Mansilla, Manuel and Ramírez Calvo, Ricardo*, La Constitución Argentina y la Obsesión Antinorteamericana, Editorial Virtudes, 2008.

[51] Concerning the USSC case law influence, Mark Tushnet describes what a 'big donor' looks like. See *Tushnet, Mark*, The New Constitutional Order, Princeton University Press, 2003.

[52] *Fallos* 32:125 (1887).

[53] *Fallos* 136:170.

[54] *Fallos* 172:29.

[55] See *Riberi, Pablo*, "Faltering Institutional Responses in Backsliding Democracies", in Riberi, Pablo (ed.), Pandemocracy in Latin America, Hart-Publishing-Bloomsbury, 2023, pp. 13–15.

[56] 290 US 398 (1934).

[57] 291 US 502 (1937).

constitutional toolkit of values, principles, and rules. Although relying on different grounds, Jonathan Miller and Carlos Rosenkrantz reject using foreign law in Argentine case law. According to these viewpoints – which I endorse – such practice has been detrimental to the country's constitutional culture. A shared view of these authors claims that Argentina has used and "abused" foreign law, particularly by resorting to the USSC case law doctrine.

Be that as it may, we are all inclined to agree on this stance. However, some of us may do so for different reasons.[58] While Professor Miller believes that U.S. law has been construed as a kind of "talisman" by Argentine courts, more leniently, Rosenkrantz argues that a non-authoritative use of foreign law may be helpful for the SCJN in Argentina.[59] I find these arguments very sound. The last one looks very appealing indeed.

Concerning Argentine constitutional culture, Miller outlined how deceiving such practices have become, particularly regarding legitimate-generating transplants. Why? Because there is a deceiving premise in this interpretative trend. Which one? Given the prestige of a foreign model, transplants are deemed as resourceful tools to instill a sense of justice and/or legitimacy to the statute or sentence at stake. Such prestige, henceforth, generates (or borrows) legitimacy from the donor's experience. Based on this fallacious premise, legitimate-generating transplants usually convey 'ad verecundiam' fallacious arguments.[60] The borrower believes that the positive effects previously observed at the former application level will also accompany the second.

II. Two Argentine Developments from a Global South Perspective

1. Argentina: The Case of the CONADEP and the Trials of the Juntas

How far should the demands for human rights standards go?

Following the return of democracy in Argentina (1983), there was an interesting and vivid academic dispute between Professor Carlos Nino and Professor Diane Orentlicher regarding human rights obligations. Orentlicher stressed the importance of analyzing Argentina's human rights accountability process under international evaluation standards. Conversely, Nino outlined the myriad concrete factors, political consequences, and democratic values at stake. Ultimately,

[58] See *Miller, Jonathan*, "The Authority of a Foreign Talisman: A Study of U.S. Constitutional Practice as Authority in Nineteenth-Century Argentina and the Argentine Elite's Leap of Faith", 46 American University Law Review (1987), p. 1483. Also see *Rosenkrantz, Carlos*, "Against Borrowing and Other Non-Authoritative Uses of Foreign Law", International Journal of Constitutional Law (Vol. 1, No. 2, April 2003), p. 223.

[59] See *Rosenkrantz, Carlos*, "Against Borrowing and Other Non-Authoritative Uses of Foreign Law", International Journal of Constitutional Law (Vol. 1, No. 2, April 2003), p. 295.

[60] See *Riberi, Pablo*, "A Constitutional Caveat: How much Legitimate Meaning Comes Along Implementing Legal Transplants?", in Rivista di Diritto Pubblico Comparato ed Europeo, Fascicolo 1 Anno 2013, pp. 101–111.

Nino's concern was whether imposing abstract and general obligations in this field – particularly overlooking Argentina's demanding historical challenges – was normatively and practically sound.[61]

I believe that resorting to these *regards croisés* provides another tool for showcasing how uncompromised deontological human rights stances originating from the Global North may misguide the observer by overshadowing the most significant and urgent political and constitutional goals that, at that moment, were jeopardizing the new democracy. Under such circumstances, I definitively endorse Professor Nino's stance. Accordingly, this case aims to present a historical event in which thorough knowledge of the underlying situation is fundamental before critically assessing the human rights policies undertaken.

Now, let me elaborate on the complex historical circumstances at stake. Although in retreat, the newly elected President had to grapple with the decisive military factor that had toppled the country's civil government for over 50 years. Acknowledging how precarious Argentine democracy was and how fragile the political, social, and economic situations were, any sensible observer would refrain from coming up with universal and unblemished human rights obligations. Indeed, human rights policies could lead to unfathomable secondary effects, so assessing the likelihood of dire consequences against those stringent deontological standards seemed reasonable.

The last Argentine dictatorship left a foreign debt of $45 billion and a crippled economy. The military government handed over power swiftly after the disaster during the Malvinas War. A pervasive sense of dismay multiplied among ordinary citizens when they came to learn that, far beyond corruption and deceit, the military government was responsible for thousands of Desaparecidos (the disappeared).[62] As Carlos Nino noted, Argentina's transmission of power was highly unusual. For transitional democracies, there were usually two modes of handing over power: either by force (as in the case of Venezuela) or by agreement (as in the case of Uruguay). Nevertheless, the Argentine transition was more akin to a "collapse". Nino expressed that "the regime loses control of a situation, leaving a vacuum that is then occupied by democratic forces".[63] The social atmosphere during this time was one of hopefulness and self-commitment. Ordinary people believed democracy would heal their wounds, creating a sense of historicalness within collective feelings.

---

[61] See *Orentlicher, Diane*, "Settling Accounts: The Duty to Prosecute Human Rights Violations of a Prior Regime", 100 Yale Law Journal (1991).

[62] During the Cold War, Argentina's military embraced the "National Security Doctrine", which was extremely popular among South America's military forces. They intended to protect the "National Being", a fundamental value constantly threatened by unknown enemies; the targets of the "*Dirty War*". Therefore, there were those people who might jeopardize the existence of this abstract concept. See *Guest, Ian*, Behind the Disappearances, University of Pennsylvania Press, 1990, pp. 257–270.

[63] Prof. Carlos Nino was a well-known scholar who served as President Alfonsin's advisor at the time.

Among other overriding concerns, after recovering democracy (1983), Argentina grappled with a dreadful legacy of gross human rights violations. Although the military remained a key factor, President Alfonsín launched a daring human rights policy aiming at two fundamental goals. On the one hand, it sought to strike a balance between the quest for memory, truth, and justice and other democratic stabilizing policies. On the other, it aimed to hold high-ranking officers accountable for heinous crimes such as killings, abductions, and torture.[64]

Accordingly, CONADEP, an independent truth commission, was appointed by President Alfonsín to pursue such goals.[65] CONADEP's report went beyond mere fact-finding; it asserted that the past dictatorship produced the most atrocious tragedy in Argentina's history.[66] The Commission emphasized that there were no mere excesses during the repression; instead, the abduction and disappearance of individuals resulted directly from what is known as a "Methodology of Terror".[67] Furthermore, to better understand the investigation's significance, CONADEP warned against isolating historical facts from the logic of the Cold War, particularly from the "National Security Doctrine", which attempted to justify past atrocities on outrageous grounds.[68]

Although the number of casualties was much higher, CONADEP identified 8,960 individuals who disappeared between 1973 and the end of the dictatorship in 1983. Women comprised 30 % of these individuals, with 3 % being pregnant at the time of their abduction. The Commission established that there were 340 detention camps. Although 5,487 petitions for habeas corpus were filed on behalf of detainees, the tribunals had granted almost any injunctions in those cases. Over 30 % of the disappeared were workers, nearly 21 % were students, 18 % were white-collar employees, 11 % were professionals, and almost 6 % were teachers. CONADEP also determined that most killings occurred between 1976 and 1978,

[64] Concerning the second goal, Jaime Malamud Goti, together with Carlos Nino, pointed out that the core guiding lines for the government were accountability, accurate fact-finding, reinforcement of universal principles of impartiality, and the general acceptance of the rule of law. These guiding lines were vital when the executive launched the 'Truth Commission: CONADEP'.

[65] According to the Argentinian Constitution's executive power provision (Article 99 § 2 CA), President Alfonsin chose fifteen respectable citizens who, independently from any public authority, had to cast light on the noxious events during the Dirty War. CONADEP had five Secretaries and a staff of sixty persons. The famous Argentine writer Ernesto Sábato chaired the CONADEP. The Commission had full investigatory powers and could demand information from the different departments of the administration. After a year of intense work, the final report was nightmarish. The public disclosure of the report, under the title of 'Nunca Más', deeply impacted society, and it became horrified by the dimension of the facts reported.

[66] See Nunca Más -Informe de la Comisión Nacional sobre la Desaparición de Personas-, Editorial Eudeba, 1994.

[67] See Nunca Más, p. 15.

[68] See Nunca Más, pp. 54–68.

with nearly 80% of the victims aged between 16 and 35 years.[69] Overall, CONADEP's final report emphasized a twofold insight that can be synthesized in the following words: First, truth is the most fundamental value, and secondly, Argentina's future generations require a collective ability to overcome this dreadful chapter of their history.

Consequently, following Alfonsín's electoral promises, both military and guerrilla leaders who had terrorized Argentine society were indicted and prosecuted. He also proposed the abrogation of draconian legislation within the criminal code, the ratification of relevant international covenants on human rights, modifications to the military's jurisdiction for ordinary crimes committed by off-duty members, the enactment of a new defense law restricting the military's role to situations of external attacks and equating the punishment for torture with that of homicide. However, President Alfonsín also proposed a statute of limitations to bar future prosecutions of those who, after following orders, had committed crimes.[70]

The new government faced political and legal challenges that overwhelmed the fragile structure of the nascent democracy. The new administration encountered opposition from unions, historically a Peronist stronghold, which, under the pretext of defending workers' rights, resisted many democratic policies undertaken by the government.[71] Additionally, some members of influential institutions, such as the Catholic Church, were reluctant to accept the cultural upheaval of that time.[72]

The new government also struggled with economic stagnation caused by a massive foreign debt that ignored the hardships of a wounded society. Financial institutions and creditors showed little concern for the immediate relief demanded by Argentina. To synthesize the government's overwhelming situation, I resort to Stotzky's. He wonders: "How does one instill in the hearts and minds of people struggling for their very existence – in the face of harsh economic realities and with the barrel of a gun in the background – that the moral bases of a democracy must be adhered to for their lives to improve?"[73]

---

[69] See Nunca Más, pp. 293–305.

[70] See *Nino, Carlos*, "The Duty to Punish Past Abuses of Human Rights Put into Context", 100 Yale Law Journal (1991), pp. 2619–2622.

[71] A new law was intended to democratize the unions. Alfonsin denounced during the campaign a backroom deal between the high-ranked military and the leaders of the C.G.T. (The centralized headquarters of the Workers' unions). So, the C.G.T., far beyond defending social rights, championed partisan political interests. For example, there were nineteen general strikes during Alfonsin's administration, while none were against President Menem's conservative policies.

[72] Article 19 of Argentina's Constitution establishes that the private actions of men that in no way harm third parties or offend the public order or morals are reserved only to God and exempted from the authority of the magistrates.

[73] *Stotzky, Irwin*, "The Fragile Bloom of democracy", 44 University of Miami Law Review (1989), pp. 106–108.

Concerning the legal and constitutional framework, Alfonsín's government faced excruciating challenges in prosecuting its leaders and holding the military accountable. Three significant obstacles hindered these prosecutions: 1) The amnesty law enacted by the military regime; 2) the military's jurisdiction established by the military code; and 3) the legal principle of "due obedience" within that code, which excused a wide range of actions otherwise punishable. Alfonsín's administration took measures to address this situation. Congress adopted the executive initiative, declaring the amnesty law null and void.[74] The second issue involved crimes committed during military service that fell under military tribunals. The government could not modify this jurisdiction with an *ex-post facto* law, as such a change would be unconstitutional.[75] The solution relied on military courts but also allowed for an automatic appeal to the Federal Court of Appeals.[76]

When General Videla challenged the constitutionality of Article 10 of Law 23049, which dealt with the new procedure, the SCJN highlighted that the Federal Appeals Court was not a "special tribunal" created to try the accused. As such, it upheld the constitutionality of the Federal Appeals Court's assumption of competence. The last controversial issue was "due obedience", which may have restricted the accountability of military officials for their past crimes. "Due obedience" was a persuasive argument that narrowed the scope of those who would be tried. However, this presumption can only excuse liabilities based on a mistake of the agent who genuinely believed in the legitimacy of the order given; otherwise, such a principle would serve as a formidable shield for delinquency.[77]

---

[74] Contradicting a historical interpretation that placed every law enacted in the country on the same level, Congress understood that the '*facto* norms' did not have the presumption of validity enjoyed by other norms enacted in times of democracy. See *Nino, Carlos*, "The Duty to Punish Past Abuses of Human Rights Put into Context", 100 Yale Law Journal (1991), p. 2625.

[75] Articles 108, 109 Argentine Military Code of Justice (M.C.J.). The principle "nullum crimen nulla poena, sine lege poenali" is stated in Argentina's Constitution as "No inhabitant of the nation may be punished without previous trial based on an earlier law than of the date of the offense, nor removed from the judges designated by the law (existing) before the date of the offense" (Article 18 CA). This provision grants that no one is bound to testify against himself and that no one can be arrested without a warrant issued by the competent judicial authority. In addition, the Constitution forbids the President from exercising judicial functions (Article 109 CA).

[76] Law 23049 established an automatic appeal if the *A-Quo Court* (Trial court) did not complete the trial within six months. In such a case, it also allowed to present new evidence in the civil tribunal if necessary.

[77] Articles 34(5), 34(6) CP (Argentine Criminal Code) exempt punishment of those who act following "due obedience" or acting in self-defense. Art. 514 M.C.J. provided, "When a crime was committed in the execution of an order of service, the superior who gave the order will be sole responsible person, and subordinate will only be considered accomplice when he has exceeded in fulfillment of that order".

Notwithstanding, Alfonsín's intention was, as Professor Nino stated, "to strike a balance between an outrageous literal interpretation, which would have established the immunity of all but the members of the juntas, and an excessively harsh interpretation, which would have unfairly required each defendant to prove positively that he was led to believe that the order was legitimate".[78] Along these lines, Alfonsín submitted a draft to Congress to exclude those who had unfettered discretion in giving orders, aiming to revoke the presumption that they had necessarily relied on the legitimacy of the orders received. Nevertheless, he also intended to secure the benefits of the principle while temporarily limiting the scope to those officers who had direct responsibility during the "Dirty War".[79]

In short, Alfonsín's government faced overwhelming pressure. He understood that he could not balance the people's demands, military obedience, and democratic requirements. Two successive mutinies demonstrated that the armed forces would not tolerate further condemnations. The rebels did not aim to seize power but sought to challenge constitutional authority. This fragile situation has had unforeseeable effects.[80]

President Alfonsín soon realized that no loyal troops could back the summoning of hundreds of suspected military officers. The overall political situation revealed a weak government unable to enforce the rule of law. The resulting political landscape had General Camps, General Menéndez, and Admiral Chamorro imprisoned, facing prosecution as perpetrators of reprehensible crimes. At the same time, because of belated trials, other officers remained free – or even on active duty – as they awaited their turn.

Alfonsín faced two uprisings by disloyal groups within the armed forces. The first rebellion occurred during Easter week of 1987. Congress, following Alfonsín's proposals, enacted the law known as "punto final" (full stop). This statute required that all indictments ought to be filed within a brief period after its promulgation. Consequently, no person could be tried if not indicted within the established statute of limitations. Conversely, this law impacted the judiciary, which increased its efforts to bring charges against five hundred military personnel. Following a second rebellion whose leaders were in Villa Martelli, Congress enacted another statute called "Ley de Obediencia Debida" ("Due Obedience Law"). This statute aimed to reduce the number of cases where low and middle-ranked militaries were involved.

---

[78] See *Nino, Carlos*, "The Duty to Punish Past Abuses of Human Rights Put into Context", 100 Yale Law Journal (1991), p. 2626.

[79] Law 23049 intended to "interpret" Due obedience (Article 514 M.C.J.). The Criminal Code also distinguishes distinct kinds of participation and liabilities in a crime. Article 45 distinguished between a crime's principal parties, instigators, and accomplices.

[80] Reading Vermeule's distinction between precautionary constitutionalism and optimizing constitutionalism may be enlightening. See *Vermeule, Adrian*, The Constitution of Risk, Cambridge University Press, 2013, pp. 27–91.

Under this provision, it was no longer possible to challenge the presumptions of legitimate understanding of an order received by lower-ranking officers during the Dirty War. The law shifted from an assumption *iuris tantum* (susceptible to challenge based on new evidence) to an assumption *iuris et de iure* (not subject to further corroboration against its given meaning). The exceptions for military ranks lacking decision-making capacities turned out to be irrebuttable.

Alfonsín's compromises were criticized as a step back from the original three-prong categories of responsibility that included those who gave orders as chief commanders, those with considerable discretion, and those who committed abhorrent crimes. The "Due Obedience Law" applied to lower-ranking officers always acting in compliance with orders and being exempt from liability.

Very dauntingly, there was a sense that the rule of law was flawed when the people noticed some responsible individuals could evade punishment. Argentines often wondered how military personnel could be excused from trial if such atrocities occurred. Under pressure, with weak social and political support, President Alfonsín teetered on the brink of a political debacle.

In 2003, with the enactment of Law 25779, the "Due Obedience", "Full Stop", and the pardons granted by President Menem and upheld by the SCJN were finally repealed by Congress. Consequently, by legally redefining these crimes as crimes against humanity, a series of new trials for military and civilian individuals involved in Argentina's illegal repression have been reopened. In this context, it is worth noting that over 310 sentences have been rendered by the courts, resulting in more than 1,100 convictions in these criminal proceedings.

No one committed to human dignity and equal justice for all can feel satisfied when impunity prevails. However, the normative assessment of these facts deserves thorough consideration. Any observer must recognize that Argentine democracy was stumbling four decades ago. Over time, the military's threat to democracy has finally vanished. Still, if we contextually consider the complex normative dimensions of the democratic transition process, those stringent and abstract deontological demands of that time lose weight.

Now, retrospectively, most Argentines were – and continue to be – proud of this historical development. A sense of fair play permeated public opinion as those trials developed according to the country's criminal law. Impunity was overcome, while the rule of law curbed retaliatory sentiments. Argentina's trials differ from the Nuremberg trials because a foreign army enforced the latter. In Argentina, there were no other soldiers than those under judicial scrutiny by their comrades. Unlike the Nuremberg trials (1945–1946) and the Colonel's trials in Greece (1975), the prosecution did not invoke general and abstract principles derived from natural law, which could be criticized as *ex post facto* norms. Accordingly, it also differed from the South African experience, where two different rules of law were at stake.

The fundamental question, which lacks a definitive answer unless we engage in counterfactuals, is whether the new democracy could have performed differently without jeopardizing the entire democratic process. Additionally, we must consider whether such a decision was legitimate at the time. This is where self-reliant Global South polities can either align with or diverge from critical assessments of the Global North. Regardless of the consequences, both *regards croisés* are on equal footing, and such criticism does not patronize the former. Conversely, my concern arises when Global North viewpoints may foil the constitutional *ethos* or potentially impair the democratic process.

2. The 'Ministerio' Case

The Inter-American System of Protection of Human Rights is over 50 years old. Established under the 'Pacto de San José de Costa Rica', the system includes the Human Rights Commission (IACHR) and the Inter-American Court of Human Rights (IACtHR). There has been a dynamic trend of decisions that endow a binding nature to all member states. Additionally, a specific "court doctrine" influences national tribunals, which, in countries like Argentina, directly applies at the domestic level through the "control of conventionality".

Argentina's and Bolivia's Constitutions grant human rights treaties the highest normative hierarchy, placing them on equal footing with the Constitution. In contrast, Costa Rica and El Salvador only award supra-legality to international treaties. Other regional Constitutions, such as Brazil's, restrict the enforcement of conventional rights to those already enumerated within the Constitution.

Therefore, Argentina, and other countries in the region are engaged in a bidimensional system for protecting human rights. One dimension is based on national Constitutions, while the other encompasses the adherent member States of the American Convention on Human Rights (ACHR).[81] Naturally, monistic or dualistic views on international law impinge upon positive or negative predispositions toward the IACtHR's increasing activism.

Global North intellectual sources influence Latin American practitioners, scholars, judges, and legislators. Noteworthy legal developments regarding human rights foundations, judicial adjudication, and judicial review have inspired such activism. There are academic trends in Latin America mirroring the so-called neo-constitutionalism. For instance, proponents of these viewpoints argue that principled activism championing the rule of law should bring about a wide range of desirable transformations in Latin America. These stances have gained momentum and thrived within the IACtHR. Furthermore, these deontological aims embraced by the IACtHR have paved the way for the *Ius Constitutionale Commune en América Latina* (ICCAL). Inspired by distinguished scholars such

[81] Since 'Velazquez v. Rodriguez' (1988), all member states are bound to enforce the Interamerican Human Rights Convention. As it happened with the European Court of Human Rights ever since Ireland v. the UK (1978), the IACtHR interpreted that there is no room for any implicit limitations when states must comply with their human rights obligations. According to article 1 of the IACHT, all member states must fulfill two duties: 1. respect human rights; 2. ensure free and whole exercise of the Charter.

as Armin von Bogdandy, the dynamic development of the ICCAL looks like a key factor for driving the Latin American mindset toward a true 'transformative constitutionalism'.[82]

Guided by the 'transformative constitutionalism' project and relying on the ICCAL as a substantive source of good law, Latin America's rule of law could be strengthened while redressing outrageous inequalities. Undoubtedly, the interplay of ICCAL and 'transformative constitutionalism' is increasingly progressing within the IACtHR's dominant neo-constitutional mindset. The IACtHR's activism has mainly been legitimized by influential academic developments emerging from the Global North.

As happened in Europe, while enshrining conventional rights, the judicial bodies empowered to enforce them cannot help but collide with domestic constitutional courts' apex authority. For example, in the case 'Ministerio' – previously known as Fontevecchia D'Amico – the IACtHR's activism regarding the American Convention on Human Rights clashed with the SCJN in Argentina.[83] In this leading case, the SCJN rendered a decision that represented a significant departure from its prior deferent doctrine. After grappling with Argentina's conventional obligations, the SCJN reinforced its interpretative powers. Although it claimed a willingness to comply with the IACtHR's sentence, in 'Ministerio', the SCJN asserted that it could neither overlook the supremacy clause of the Argentine constitution nor forfeit its authority to exercise judicial review.

In the original case, Fontevecchia D'Amico, the IACtHR declared that Argentina had violated the petitioners' right to freedom of expression (as provided in Article 13 of the American Convention on Human Rights). The IACtHR ordered Argentina to comply with the following obligations: 1) to annul the civil sentence imposed on Fontevecchia and D'Amico; 2) to publish a summary of the IACtHR's sentence on the SCJN's website, the Official State Gazette, and in a national newspaper of massive circulation; and 3) to award economic reparations to the petitioners, including reimbursement of amounts awarded to Fontevecchia and D'Amico.

What was the Argentine SCJN's reaction to this decision? After a detailed analysis of it, SCJN complied with items 'b' and 'c' of the IACtHR's sentence. However, the SCJN refused to enforce the item 'a'. Although it was not a unanimous ruling of the Tribunal, this reluctance appears to be an uncompromised limit set by SCJN. The sentence reflects a majority vote dismissing the claim issued by Justices Lorenzetti, Highton de Nolasco, and Rosenkrantz, while Justice Rosatti, who shared the majority's *dictum*, wrote his own opinion. Finally, Justice Maqueda dissented.

---

[82] See *von Bogdandy, Armin*, Por un Derecho Común para América Latina, Siglo XXI Editores, 2020, pp. 51–97.

[83] See CSJ 368/1998 (34-M)/CS1 Ministerio de Relaciones Exteriores y Culto / informe sentencia dictada en el caso 'Fontevecchia y D'Amico vs. Argentina' por la Corte Interamericana de Derechos Humanos (IACtHR). The sentence was issued on February 14, 2017.

The 'Ministerio' case resumed Argentina's long-standing constitutional tradition, which asserts that treaties must be construed under public law principles (e.g., the supremacy of the national Constitution). To understand this case correctly, exploring the underlying normative framework is appealing to the Argentine Constitution of 1853, following Alberdi's core insights, proposed not only a scheme of rules but also endorsed guiding principles drawn from the Constitution itself.[84] In this sense, Article 27 of the Constitution provides: "The Federal Government is under the obligation to strengthen its relationships of peace and trade with foreign powers, by means of treaties in accordance with the principles of public law laid down by this Constitution."

This provision provides an interpretative guide for the courts concerning international law and foreign relations. According to SCJN, Article 27 takes center stage as a sphere of sovereign reserve, providing a margin of national appreciation, as expressly underscored by Justice Rosatti. The principles of public law to which treaties must conform are binding on the SCJN and cannot be overlooked. While Article 27 mandates the nation to engage in international relations to promote commerce and peace, whatever the content of international law, it must not override such public law constitutional principles.

Besides, another fundamental provision regarding human rights treaties and international covenants should not be neglected. According to a new section incorporated during the last amendment of 1994, the second part of Article 75, section 22 of the Constitution provides: "[...] in the full force of their provisions, they have the highest constitutional hierarchy, do not repeal any section of the First Part of this Constitution, and are to be understood as complementing the rights and guarantees recognized herein." The majority opinion in 'Ministerio' explicitly leans on Article 75, paragraph 22, emphasizing that treaties with maximum constitutional hierarchy must be enforced without repealing any article of the first part of the national Constitution.

Therefore, regarding the conflicting constructions between the IACtHR and the SCJN, the 'Ministerio' case represented an upheaval of the SCJN's previous doctrine. The SCJN challenged the scope of the IACtHR's decision and reconsidered its self-restraint when the constitutional supremacy clause was at stake. In 'Ministerio,' the SCJN advocates for a harmonious interpretation of the American Convention; otherwise, the IACtHR would effectively become a reviewing or cassation instance for all member states' final constitutional decisions.[85]

---

[84] It is worth noticing that article 28 CA established: "The principles, guarantees, and rights recognized in the preceding article shall not be modified by the laws that regulate their enforcement", while article 33 is also clearly coherent, which broadens the constitutional protection of other "*non-enumerated*" individual rights if they are compatible with popular sovereignty and the republican form of government.

[85] See *Ábalos, María Gabriela*, "Control de constitucionalidad y de convencionalidad sobre una decisión interamericana", La Ley -Suplemento Derecho Constitucional-, March 2017.

Justice Rosenkrantz stressed that "the judgments of the Inter-American Court, issued in contentious proceedings against the Argentine State, are – in principle – mandatory, are – in principle – of mandatory compliance", emphasizing that 'such mandatory nature, however, only applies to the judgments issued by the international tribunal within the framework of its remedial powers'. According to his opinion, the *dictum* of this case does not deny the binding nature of the IACtHR's decisions. This is so because following article 68.1 of the Charter, the binding nature of such decisions must be limited to the matter over which the international court has jurisdiction (articles 63 ICHR; and articles 27, 75, inc. 22 and 108, 116, 117 CA). Rosenkrantz finally emphasized that this has always been the scope upon which Argentina has internationally bound itself to abide by the American Convention on Human Rights.[86]

The majority opinion also stated that one of the most cherished principles of Argentine public law is the overriding character of the Supreme Court's decisions: head of the Judiciary Power (Article 108 CA). It also underscored the importance of the *res judicata* character of its unalterable decisions as an overriding principle. Justice Rosenkrantz's separate opinion stressed that the Inter-American Court of Human Rights could not *"render ineffective"* a judgment issued by the SCJN, assimilating the idea of "rendering ineffective" to that of "revoking the sentence".[87] In the same vein, Justice Rosatti agreed with the majority opinion that the IACtHR's decision not only went beyond its specific and proper attributions.

The sentence also championed the need for a harmonious interpretation by the IACtHR *vis à vis* the SCJN – the highest Tribunal of the Argentine judiciary system. Otherwise, as the sentence holds, the IACtHR would become a reviewing body or transform itself into a reviewing instance that would be at odds with the coadjutant and complementary nature of the Interamerican system. Furthermore, the IACtHR's decision would be in blatant contradiction to the Preamble of the *Pacto de San José de Costa Rica*. As regards the national decision, Justice Rosatti shares the opinion that it is not possible to admit the formal revocation sought without violating the provisions of articles 27 and 75, paragraph 22, of the Argentine Constitution.[88]

The holding of 'Ministerio' also invites the IACtHR to enhance "courts' dialogue" by fostering decisional convergence as contingent national and international spheres may overlap. Furthermore, Justice Rosatti argued for a 'margin of appreciation' in favor of domestic courts, which are bound to enforce the Ameri-

---

[86] See *Pittier, Lautaro*, "The control of conventionality and the national margin of appreciation", La Ley -Suplemento Derecho Constitucional-, November 2019, p. 7.

[87] For further comments, see *Ábalos, María Gabriela,* "Control de constitucionalidad y de convencionalidad sobre una decisión interamericana", La Ley -Suplemento Derecho Constitucional-, March 2017.

[88] See *Pittier, Lautaro*, "The control of conventionality and the national margin of appreciation", La Ley -Suplemento Derecho Constitucional-, November 2019, p. 7.

can Convention on Human Rights. The majority vote finally stressed that both organs, whose roles aim to settle conflicts in the national and the international spheres, must be the ultimate interpreters of their respective competencies.[89]

Finally, let me share a comprehensive assessment of the current situation. In my opinion, we must not lose sight that it has yielded outstanding human rights decisions against impunity, expiry laws, and amnesties concerning the right to an investigation of gross violation of human rights[90], the right to an effective recourse, and due process[91]; the right of Indigenous people and non-discrimination. All these interpretative trends are major normative hallmarks for improving the rule of law in Latin America. Naturally, my criticism does not challenge the idea that the legacy of IACtHR has definitively improved all these dimensions.

Notwithstanding, there are other things at stake. For example, it is also true that SCJN has endorsed IACtHR's activism for years. Since "Giroldi" (1995), the Argentine Highest Tribunal has construed that all case law delivered by the IACtHR – even by its holdings or *ratio-decidendi* – is compellingly enforceable in the country.[92] Furthermore, beyond its involvement, not only every IACtHR's ruling but also its 'advisory opinions', must be abided by the country. Concerning the 'control of conventionality', for many years, the SCJN has upheld a deferent doctrine aligned with the IACtHR's increasing activism. However, in countries of the region, after the "Gelman v. Uruguay" case, this tendency has undergone strong criticism. In summary, there has been little institutional dialogue between domestic courts and the IACtHR. If there was any, it has been a top-down monologue.

Autochthonous constitutional developments must stand on equal footing. This is why judges, political activists, and scholars who had endorsed a polymorphism of sources for human rights could not help feeling uneasiness when the IACtHR's unfettered activism undermined the enabling constitutional rules that had paved the way for their authority. Ultimately, what troubles me is that such untamed activism impairs the constitutional *ethos* that has allowed countries like Argentina to engage and enhance a double-pronged human rights protection system.

---

[89] See *Ábalos, María Gabriela*, "Control de constitucionalidad y de convencionalidad sobre una decisión interamericana", La Ley -Suplemento Derecho Constitucional-, March 2017.

[90] E.g.: Gómez Lund in Brazil (2010), Almonacid Arellano in Chile (2006), or the 'Simón case' in Argentina (2003). Concerning 'impunity', Barrios Altos on 'self-amnesty law' in Peru (1995) and the latest decision of the IACtHR in the case Vega González y Otro v. Chile deserve attention. On September 26, 2024, the IACtHR's decision condemned Chile for complying with its domestic Criminal Code instead of upholding the IACtHR's consolidated doctrine against impunity in gross violation of human rights. Said provision provides a gradual prescription in favor of some repressors.

[91] The SCJN's 'Daniel López case' (2004) and Herrera Ulloa v. Costa Rica (2006).

[92] The 'Giroldi case' refers to a ruling by the Argentine Court of Justice on the admissibility of an 'extraordinary recourse'. The SCJN's sentence was issued on April 7, 1995.

E. Closing Remarks

These historical lessons demonstrate that, concerning comparative constitutional law, an introspective approach can be intellectually rewarding when grappling with Latin American constitutional challenges. They also reveal that, beyond pluralism, engaging with contextual and structural normative analysis provides adaptative tools to hammer out those concrete challenges.

I have underlined that from a deep Global South perspective – specifically from Latin America and, more concretely, from Argentina – the alternative of conflictive *regards croisés* allows us to connect the dots between the Global North's hegemonic influence and the resulting Global South's weakened constitutional *ethos*. Accordingly, I share Justice Carlos Rosenkrantz's take on this as he noted: "We should relate foreign law as workers relate to scaffolds. That is, as artifacts they step on to enhance and facilitate their own constructive abilities, but that are never components of their final work and never determinants of the shape of what is constructed".[93]

This text's core aim is to underscore the importance of strengthening Latin American constitutional developments, particularly those thriving in Argentina. It does not intend to criticize the Global North's normative contributions. However, it raises an unavoidable concern that, whatever their content, they always loom hegemonic.

In cases of clashing *regards croisés*, my focus is to advance a comprehensive analysis of their lingering effects in Latin America, especially in Argentina. This analysis and the historical cases presented highlight the necessity of developing a robust constitutional *ethos*. Rather than resorting to mere imitation, polities of the Global South must engage in shaping an indigenous sense of normative priorities.[94] If this holds, comparativist observers may also uncover another concealed drawback in Latin American faltering democracies: Both ruling elites and the people at large often struggle to distinguish between constitutional politics and ordinary politics.[95] In my opinion this has been the most overriding hurdle for Latin American constitutional polities.

Among the various constitutional systems in the region, comparative constitutional law and international human rights law have undoubtedly served as fundamental sources of legitimacy. These frameworks have not only consoli-

---

[93] See *Rosenkrantz, Carlos*, "Against Borrowing and Other Non-Authoritative Uses of Foreign Law", International Journal of Constitutional Law (Vol. 1, No. 2, April 2003), p. 295.

[94] *Tushnet, Mark*, "Can there be autonomous methods of constitutional interpretation?", in Gardós-Orosz, Fruzsina and Szente, Zoltán (eds.), Populist Challenges to Constitutional Interpretation in Europe and Beyond, Routledge, 2021, p. 64.

[95] *Riberi, Pablo*, "Populist and non-democratic reading of the Constitution – Sad lessons from Latin America", in Gardós-Orosz, Fruzsina and Szente, Zoltán (eds.), Populist Challenges to Constitutional Interpretation in Europe and Beyond, Routledge, 2021, p. 310.

dated multidimensional human rights protection mechanisms but have also strengthened democratic transitional processes. Beyond the normative content of the disputes, the cases presented here illustrate how the Global North's hegemonic influence has affected the development of a self-reliant constitutional culture.

In conclusion, I wish to underscore two of the most fundamental intuitions of this text: the importance of pluralism and stringent introspection when grappling with comparative constitutional law. To emphasize this insight, I will lean on Hannah Arendt's concept of "thinking without a banister" or "groundless thinking". Although she aimed to envision how we are to navigate in this time of collective puzzlement – expressing a sense of loss in terms of historicalness – her metaphor conveys that "as you go up and down the stairs, you can always hold on to the banister so that you do not fall. But we have lost the banister. That is the way I tell it myself"; Arendt affirms.[96]

Drawing from her insightful statement, I emphasize that the ever-faltering constitutional *ethos* in the Global South, particularly in Latin America and Argentina, has learned that Global North's hegemonic sources seldom represent a reliable banister. Naturally, they can provide inspiring lessons and enlightening examples. In other words, they can represent a flight in a single run of steps connecting to others by landings, which, more comprehensively, make up the complete staircase.

[96] See *Arendt, Hannah*, "Hannah Arendt on Hannah Arendt", in Thinking without a Banister -Essays in Understanding 1953–1975–, Schocken Books, 2018, p. 473.

Constitutionalism in Asia – A few broad strokes on a large canvas

Surya Deva

A. Introduction

Comparing constitutions 'requires us to consider differences (and similarities) in forms of government as well as the normative philosophies behind constitutional choices.'[1] The task of comparison – especially within the length of a paper – becomes arduous if differences among the objects of comparison are too stark. The Asian continent is a case in point. It is very difficult to draw some common trends about constitutional law or constitutionalism in Asia because Asia is very heterogeneous not only in terms of its geography but also in relation to political, economic, social and cultural conditions. It also features diverse legal systems: in addition to civil law and common law systems, Asia has countries with hybrid legal systems. Moreover, religious laws as well as customary or Indigenous laws are an integral part of constitutional governance in some Asian countries.[2] Asia is the only world region with no regional human rights instrument or institution – something that explains the challenges of building consensus around issues of common interest.

At the same time, how constitutions operate, or do not operate, in Asia matters significantly to global constitutionalism and the entire world generally. Asia is the home to 60 percent of the world's population. It also features the world's largest democracy as well as the largest single-party authoritarian regime. Moreover, Asia is the site of a major geo-political divide involving two emerging world powers (China and India). This has a direct effect on how the Western torchbearers of constitutionalism engage – whether through intervention or acquiescence – with constitutional developments in Asia. Finally, the military continues to play a vital extra-constitutional role in several Asian countries, even during peaceful times. Some of these factors perhaps explain why constitutionalism in

---

[1] *Roger Masterman* and *Robert Schütze*, 'Introduction' in Roger Masterman and Robert Schütze (eds.), The Cambridge Companion to Comparative Constitutional Law (Cambridge University Press, 2019) 1.

[2] Constitutions of certain Asian countries expressly embrace an official religion. For example, Article 3 of the Malaysian Constitution states that 'Islam is the religion of the Federation, but other religions can also be practiced safely and peacefully in any part of the Federation'.

Asia, and the Global South generally, is receiving greater attention from scholars in the last decade.[3]

With these caveats, this paper attempts to offer some common themes in the field of constitutional law and constitutionalism in Asia. These themes are not intended to be exhaustive. Rather, the goal is to paint a broad stroke picture giving glimpses into constitutional histories, political ideologies, key governance institutions and selected constitutionalism principles. Part B of the paper unpacks the following five themes: decolonised nationalism, constitutional self-empowerment, co-opting mechanisms of checks and balances, constitutionalism on streets, caged courts and transformative constitutionalism. Part C offers concluding remarks.

B. Key Trends

I. Decolonised nationalism

Many countries in Asia experienced colonisation from the British, Dutch, French, Portuguese or Spanish powers, both public and private. For example, the British East India Company, which obtained a charter from the Queen in 1600 to conduct trade in the Indian Ocean region, ended up exercising political power over India and at one point in time had more armed forces than the British army.[4]

While the freedom from colonial rulers after the Second World War provided an opportunity to these Asian countries to break from the past, the constitution making process was influenced by colonial concepts, principles and understandings. We can take a few examples from India to illustrate this point. After India's independence in 1947, the Constituent Assembly decided to opt for a parliamentary form of government because of its familiarity with the cabinet government[5] and the practice and traditions that evolved during the British rule.[6] Shri K M Munshi, one of the prominent members of the Assembly, explained the reasons why India opted for a parliamentary form of government:

---

[3] See, for example, *Daniel Bonilla Maldonado* (ed.), Constitutionalism of the Global South (Cambridge University Press, 2013); *Rosalind Dixon* and *Tom Ginsburg* (eds.), Comparative Constitutional Law in Asia (Edward Elgar, 2014); *Albert Chen* (ed.), Constitutionalism in Asia in the Early Twenty-First Century (Cambridge University Press, 2014); *Philipp Dann, Michael Riegner* and *Maxim Bönnemann* (eds.), The Global South and Comparative Constitutional Law (Oxford University Press, 2020); *David S Law, Holning Lau* and *Alex Schwartz* (eds.), The Oxford Handbook of Constitutional Law in Asia (Oxford University Press, 2023).

[4] See *William Dalrymple*, The Anarchy: The Relentless Rise of the East India Company (Bloomsbury, 2019).

[5] *Granville Austin*, The Indian Constitution: Cornerstone of a Nation, (Oxford: Clarendon Press, 1966) 116.

[6] *B Shiva Rao*, The Framing of India's Constitution – A Study, (New Delhi: The Indian Institute of Public Administration, 1968) 334.

'We must not forget a very important fact that during the last one hundred years Indian public life has largely drawn upon the tradition of the British constitutional law. Most of us, and during the last several generations before us, public men in India, have looked up to the British model as the best. … Our constitutional traditions have become parliamentary …'[7]

Almost all constitutions in Asia have fundamental rights provisions. It is interesting to note that several of these constitutions make a distinction between civil and political rights on the one hand and social, economic and cultural rights on the other. Such a distinction is made in many Western constitutional traditions in the sense that civil and political rights of individuals are accorded a priority. Although the leaders of the Indian independence movement drew no distinction between the positive and negative obligations of the state in relation to fundamental rights,[8] the Indian Constituent Assembly separated fundamental rights in Part III (civil and political rights) from the directive principles of state policy in Part IV (social, economic and cultural rights) on the ground of justiciability.[9] Similarly, most Asian constitutions enshrine a state-centric notion of fundamental rights, again closer to the Western tradition in which fundamental rights are seen as a shield against the state power. This was so despite power in Asian societies being vested also in a range of private actors such as *zamindars* (landowners) and religious leaders.[10]

In the last few decades, politicians, policy makers and scholars in Asia have made a case for decolonising constitutions by embracing Indigenous constitutional governance concepts. However, it seems that the decolonisation project in Asia is being hijacked by nationalist forces. Elliott makes a distinction between 'civic' and 'authoritarian' nationalism and argues that historically 'nationalism was considered to be a force of progress, as scores of people who developed national identities rose against colonial powers to form their own nations.'[11] However, the nationalist narrative could also be exploited by political leaders to undermine liberal constitutional values.

[7] VII *Constituent Assembly Debates* 984–985.

[8] *Austin*, note 5, 52.

[9] For the relevance of the justiciability distinction between Part III and Part IV rights, see *M P Singh*, 'The Statics and the Dynamics of the Fundamental Rights and the Directive Principles: A Human Rights Perspective' (2003) 5 Supreme Court Cases (Journal) 1.

[10] The Indian Constitution of 1950 is an exception to this in that it expressly extends the protection of certain fundamental rights against private actors. Austin cites three provisions, i.e., articles 15(2), 17 and 23 which have been 'designed to protect the individual against the action of other private citizen'. Austin, note 5, 51. However, it is arguable that the protection of even articles 24 and 29(1) could be invoked against private individuals. See *Vijayashri Sripati*, 'Toward Fifty Years of Constitutionalism and Fundamental Rights in India: Looking Back to See Ahead (1950–2000)' (1998) 14 American University International Law Review 413, 447–448.

[11] *Amitai Etzioni*, '"Good" vs "Bad" Nationalism in Asia' (23 September 2019), https://thediplomat.com/2019/09/good-vs-bad-nationalism-in-asia/ (All internet sources were last accessed on April 9, 2025 and were up-to-date at that time).

Taking India as an example, Roux notes that 'an ethno-nationalist account of Hindu governance traditions is currently being used to contest the authentic Indianness of the 1950 Constitution and to oppress the Muslim minority in that country.'[12] In fact, the Indian Constitution embraces

> 'A new model of secularism – not the secularism of the French or American constitutions, but in effect a vision of guaranteeing the political equality of all Indian religions, which implied the need for governmental policies to fight religious fanaticism and to correct the imbalances of power within and among different religions.'[13]

However, this decolonised vision of secularism is coming under attack from the winds of nationalism in India, as religious minorities are living in the shadow of the majority Hindu religion and hence not enjoying a *de facto* equality to practice their religious practices.[14]

One can also see the debate concerning attempts to portray India as 'Bharat' in this context,[15] though it is worth noting that the Indian Constitution uses both terms in Article 1.[16] It also seems that linguistic nationalism is resurfacing in India,[17] a country that has long been celebrated for managing linguistic diversities through a complex constitutional design.[18] Article 29 of the Constitution provides: 'Any section of the citizens residing in the territory of India or any part thereof having a distinct language, script or culture of its own shall have the right to conserve the same.' Linguistic minorities also have 'the right to establish and administer educational institutions of their choice' (Article 30). Moreover, while Article 343 provides that the official language of the central government shall be Hindi, the same provision permits the use of English for all the official purposes of the central government. English is also prescribed as 'the official language for

[12] *Theunis Roux*, 'The Global South Critique of Liberal Constitutionalism' (5 November 2024), https://www.auspublaw.org/blog/2024/11/the-global-south-critique-of-liberal-constitutionalism.

[13] *Debasish Roy Chowdhury* and *John Keane*, To kill a democracy: India's passage to despotism (Oxford University Press, 2021) 11.

[14] *S Khan*, 'Vulnerabilities of Religious Minorities in India: Unmasking the Impact of Rising Hindu Nationalism' (18 August 2023), https://www.internationalaffairs.org.au/australianoutlook/vulnerabilities-of-religious-minorities-in-india-unmasking-the-impact-of-rising-hindu-nationalism/.

[15] John Elliott, 'Bharat or India? Narendra Modi reopens an old debate' (13 September 2023), https://www.commonwealthroundtable.co.uk/commonwealth/eurasia/india/bharat-or-india-narendra-modi-reopens-an-old-debate/.

[16] Article 1(1) of the Constitution reads: 'India, that is Bharat, shall be a Union of States.'

[17] *Hannah Ellis-Petersen*, '"A threat to unity": Anger over push to make Hindi national language of India' (25 December 2022), https://www.theguardian.com/world/2022/dec/25/threat-unity-anger-over-push-make-hindi-national-language-of-india *Afreen Hussain*, 'The battle against Hindi imposition: Why Tamil Nadu won't back down' (7 March 2025), https://www.indiatoday.in/india/tamil-nadu/story/tamil-nadu-hindi-imposition-autonomy-federalism-nep-2690578-2025-03-07.

[18] See *Sujit Choudhry*, 'Managing linguistic nationalism through constitutional design: Lessons from South Asia' (2009) 7:4 International Journal of Constitutional Law 577.

communication' between two states or between a state and the central government (Article 346). The Eighth Schedule of the Constitution recognises 22 languages. At the same time, several constitutional provisions encourage the progressive use of Hindi and/or restrict the use of English (e.g., Articles 120(2), 344 and 351).

Despite such a constitutional intent, it appears that the project of decolonising India from English is being used as an excuse to push for Hindi nationalism. The Education Minister's reasoning makes this clear: while there is 'no question of imposing any language', there is an 'over-reliance on foreign languages, limiting students' exposure to linguistic roots' and that the new National Education Policy is trying to correct this.[19]

One can see similar nationalism trends elsewhere in Asia.[20] For example, the Chinese government is actively promoting Putonghua throughout the country as part of a narrative of cultural identity and political unity,[21] because ethnic minority languages can be perceived as a 'problem' at regional levels.[22] This means that the dialects or languages of ethnic minorities are getting sidelined as part of nationalism. During debates about how the National Security Law may undermine the constitutionally guaranteed autonomy enjoyed by Hong Kong under its Basic Law, one could again see glimpses of constitutional nationalism at play. Hongkongers, including students and lawmakers, are now expected to 'love

---

[19] '"No Question Of Imposing Language But..." Education Minister In Hindi Row' (21 February 2025), https://www.ndtv.com/india-news/hindi-imposition-row-tamil-nadu-national-education-policy-3-language-formula-no-question-of-imposition-centre-on-hindi-row-with-tamil-nadu-7760460.

[20] See, for example, *Giorgio Shani* and *Takashi Kibe* (eds.), Religion and Nationalism in Asia (Routledge, 2020).

[21] The volume edited by Leibold and Chen explores complexities concerning striking a balance between unity and diversity as well as how actual practices are different from projected policies in terms of minority education. *James Leibold* and *Chen Yangbin* (eds.), Minority education in China: Balancing unity and diversity in an era of critical pluralism (Hong Kong University Press, 2014).

[22] Yao et al, for example, note that 'the policy support for Uyghur language education has been continuously tightened due to growing ethnic tensions and fears of separatism. For example, local schools were required to change the instructional language from Uyghur to Mandarin Chinese …; ethnic minority schools were recommended to merge with Mandarin-Chinese-medium-of-instruction schools …; and all schools were instructed to offer Mandarin Chinese language classes from the first year of primary education.' *Jiazhou Yao*, *Marianne Turner* and *Gary Bonar*, 'Ethnic minority language policies and practices in China: revisiting Ruiz's language orientation theory through a critical biliteracy lens' (2024) 45 Journal of Multilingual and Multicultural Development 2400, 2404.

China' (or 'love the motherland'),[23] which in practice includes an expectation not to criticise the existing Chinese constitutional or political system.

II. Constitutional self-empowerment

Many governments in Asia have invoked constitutional provisions to enhance their power. While at times this was done by adopting a particular interpretation of a constitutional provision, constitutions were also amended to expand power or ensure its concentration. There have also been occasions where constitutions were suspended to usurp power. All these traits are reflective of what I will call 'constitutional self-empowerment', that is, an improper use of constitutional provisions to expand or entrench power beyond permissible boundaries.[24]

Constitutional provisions have been used to impose emergency for political reasons, e.g., by Mrs Indira Gandhi in 1975 in India on the pretext of maintaining peace and security of the country. During the emergency, Mrs Gandhi introduced the 42nd Constitutional Amendment which tried to curtail courts' judicial review power and expanded the parliament's power to amend the Constitution. Similarly, in November 2007, General Pervez Musharraf imposed an 'emergency rule' in Pakistan – thereby suspending the Constitution and dismissing the Supreme Court – on the ground that drastic measures were necessary to combat a terrorist threat.[25] In 2018, President Xi got the Chinese Constitution amended to remove the two-term limit for presidents.[26] This removal of limit is quite significant because there are not many other checks and balances within the Chinese constitutional or political system.

A more creative method of constitutional self-empowerment is when a constitutional provision is interrupted to enhance one's power. Notably, this has been done both by the judiciary and the executive in India. A good example of the

---

[23] 'Hong Kong primary pupils must understand constitution, secondary students must "love motherland" under new values curriculum' (30 November 2021), https://www.scmp.com/news/hong-kong/education/article/3157933/hong-kong-primary-pupils-must-understand-constitution; *James Griffiths*, 'Hong Kong's new loyalty oath requires all lawmakers to love China – and the Communist Party' (24 February 2021), https://edition.cnn.com/2021/02/23/asia/hong-kong-patriots-election-intl-hnk/index.html.

[24] Constitutional self-empowerment is distinct from but complementary to what Dawood terms 'partisan self-dealing': a phenomenon in which 'political actors craft election laws in order to entrench themselves in power. Electoral rules that govern voting, political parties, electoral boundaries, apportionment, the administration of elections, and campaign finance are often designed to achieve partisan objectives.' *Yasmin Dawood*, 'Electoral Fairness and the Law of Democracy: A Structural Rights Approach to Judicial Review' (2012) 62 University of Toronto Law Journal 499, 500.

[25] *Open Society Foundation*, 'Emergency Rule and Protests in Pakistan' (11 September 2007), https://www.opensocietyfoundations.org/voices/emergency-rule-and-protests-pakistan.

[26] 'China's Xi allowed to remain "president for life" as term limits removed' (11 March 2018), https://www.bbc.com/news/world-asia-china-43361276.

former is the Supreme Court's interpretation of the term 'consultation' in Article 124 of the Indian Constitution[27] as 'concurrence'.[28] By this interpretation, the Court – contrary to the intent of the constitution makers – wrested the power of appointing judges from the executive and became a self-appointing judiciary. To overcome this interpretation, the Indian government brought a constitutional amendment to establish a National Judicial Appointments Commission which was envisaged to make recommendations to the President for the appointment of judges. However, the Court has struck down this constitutional amendment.[29]

An example of the latter is provided by the August 2019 Orders of the Indian President – the Constitution (Application to Jammu and Kashmir) Order 2019,[30] and the Declaration under Article 370(3) of the Constitution[31] – coupled with the Jammu and Kashmir Reorganisation Act 2019 (JKR Act), which took away the special constitutional status and autonomy of Jammu and Kashmir conferred by Article 370 of the Constitution. The most notable aspect of this development was that the government used creative ways to achieve this constitutional outcome without amending Article 370, something that should not have been possible on the face of it.[32]

One can find such examples beyond India as well. The use of interpretation power by the Chinese National People's Congress' Standing Committee (NPCSC) in relation to the Basic Law of Hong Kong is a case in point. Article 158 of the Basic Law stipulates that the NPCSC has the final power to interpret the Basic Law. In August 2014, the NPCSC issued a decision concerning both the selection of the Chief Executive by universal suffrage and the formation of the Legislative Council in 2016.[33] This decision, along with the 2004 NPCSC interpretation, undermines Hong Kong's high degree of autonomy by making the

---

[27] Article 124(2) reads: 'Every Judge of the Supreme Court shall be appointed by the President by warrant under his hand and seal after consultation with such of the Judges of the Supreme Court and of the High Court in the States as the President may deem necessary for the purpose.'

[28] *S C Advocates on Record Association v Union of India* AIR 1994 SC 268; *In re, Presidential Reference* AIR 1999 SC 1.

[29] *Supreme Court Advocates-on-Record Association v Union of India* AIR 2016 SC 117.

[30] See https://egazette.gov.in/(S(jx5c0wuty3yjqhceoghbcpoi))/ViewPDF.aspx.

[31] See https://egazette.gov.in/(S(jx5c0wuty3yjqhceoghbcpoi))/ViewPDF.aspx. This order was pursuant to a resolution adopted by Rajya Sabha, the Upper House of the parliament: https://pib.gov.in/newsite/PrintRelease.aspx?relid=192487.

[32] See *Surya Deva*, 'Constitutional Politics over (Un)Constitutional Amendments: The Indian Experience' in Rehan Abeyratne and Ngoc Son Bui (eds.), Law and Politics of Unconstitutional Constitutional Amendments in Asia (Abingdon: Routledge, 2021) 189.

[33] *NPCSC*, 'Decision of the Standing Committee of the National People's Congress on Issues Relating to the Selection of the Chief Executive of the Hong Kong Special Administrative Region by Universal Suffrage and on the Method for Forming the Legislative Council of the Hong Kong Special Administrative Region in the Year 2016', http://www.2017.gov.hk/filemanager/template/en/doc/20140831a.pdf.

Basic Law's goal of achieving universal suffrage a mirage.[34] The NPCSC not only introduced a new five-step process – not found in the Basic Law – as a pre-condition to make any incremental changes towards achieving universal suffrage, but also glossed over a critical distinction between reporting for 'approval' the method of selecting Hong Kong's Chief Executive (Annex I of the Basic Law) and reporting for 'record' the method for the formation of the Legislative Council (Annex II of the Basic Law).

III. Co-opting mechanisms of checks and balances

There are many ways to undermine constitutionalism or democracy for that matter. Some of these ways can be described as 'crude' in that they involve overt and/or violent acts such as a coup to overthrow a government or a constitution. Coups 'involve an attempt to seize executive power and entail a concrete, observable and illegal action by military or civilian personnel.'[35] Several Asian countries have experienced coups, e.g., Bangladesh, Fiji, Indonesia, Myanmar, Nepal, Pakistan, South Korea and Thailand.[36] General Prayuth Chan-o-cha, who led the coup in Thailand in 2014, is still in charge, while the 2021 coup disrupted Myanmar's transition to democracy.[37] However, some coups – labelled as 'self-coups' – are led by an incumbent executive leader and are aimed at illegally extending one's term in office or targeting the other two government wings (legislature and judiciary).[38] The declaration of martial law by South Korean President Yoon Suk-yeol in early December 2024 illustrates this phenomenon, though the President was forced to overturn the declaration just six hours later.[39]

Other ways to undermine constitutionalism are more 'clever' for they involve sophisticated approaches to achieve anti-constitutional goals. Capturing or co-opting various institutions and mechanisms that are meant to exert checks and balances over the executive is one such approach. Independent courts are often regarded as a bulwark against abuse of power by the government. In addition, the 'fourth branch' government institutions concerning human rights, anti-corrup-

[34] See *Surya Deva*, 'Threats to Hong Kong's Autonomy from the NPC's Standing Committee: The Role of Courts and the Basic Structure Doctrine' (2020) 50 Hong Kong Law Journal 901.

[35] *John Joseph Chin and Joe Wright,* 'What is a self-coup? South Korea president's attempt ended in failure – A notable exception in a growing global trend' (6 December 2024), https://theconversation.com/what-is-a-self-coup-south-korea-presidents-attempt-ended-in-failure-a-notable-exception-in-a-growing-global-trend-235738.

[36] *Ankit Panda*, 'A Brief History of the Coup d'État in the Asia-Pacific' (18 July 2016), https://thediplomat.com/2016/07/a-brief-history-of-the-coup-detat-in-the-asia-pacific/.

[37] *Nicholas Farrelly*, 'Lessons from Coup-Making in Southeast Asia' (12 February 2021), https://www.internationalaffairs.org.au/australianoutlook/lessons-from-coup-making-in-southeast-asia/.

[38] *Chin* and *Wright*, note 35.

[39] *E Tammy Kim*, 'A Coup, Almost, in South Korea' (4 December 2024), https://www.newyorker.com/news/the-lede/a-coup-almost-in-south-korea.

tion and elections play a key role in controlling the executive powers and in turn promote constitutionalism.[40] The role of free media and civil society is equally vital in this respect.

We can see this clever approach being employed by governments in several Asian countries. We can take national human rights institutions (NHRIs) as a case in point. Independent NHRIs, acting in accordance with the Paris Principles,[41] operate as a check on the abuse of power by the government. The Global Alliance of National Human Rights Institutions reviews and provides accreditation to NHRIs whether they meet the Paris Principles fully (A status) or partially (B status).[42] Out of 29 NHRIs from the Asia and the Pacific, only 18 have an 'A' status.[43] Moreover, doubts are expressed about the *in practice* (as opposed to *on paper*) independence[44] of even some A status NHRIs.[45] The compromised status of NHRIs is directly due to some governments in Asia trying to use NHRIs as their legitimisation puppets. The following overall assessment of NHRIs in Asia by an Asian network of CSOs is quite telling:

> 'In some countries, NHRIs struggled with securing basic safeguards to function independently and in others, despite having those mandates, NHRIs failed to carry them out independently. While in some countries, governments' attempts to limit NHRIs' work and functioning continued by way of reduced budgets or interference, there was also a recurring trend of a lack of a transparent, merit-based process in the selection and appointment of NHRIs' commissioners. In some other countries, political turmoil rendered some NHRIs either dissolved or subsumed under authoritarian regimes, even using them as a way to advance their agenda and validate their legitimacy.'[46]

In addition to NHRIs, some Asian governments have also tried to undermine the independence of election commissions to gain an unfair advantage during elections. Commenting on the incremental castigation of the Indian Election Commission, Jain concludes:

---

[40] See *Mark Tushnet*, The New Fourth Branch: Institutions for Protecting Constitutional Democracy (Cambridge University Press, 2021).

[41] 'Principles relating to the Status of National Institutions (The Paris Principles)' GA Res 48/134 (20 December 1993), https://www.ohchr.org/en/instruments-mechanisms/instruments/principles-relating-status-national-institutions-paris.

[42] See https://ganhri.org/accreditation/.

[43] See https://ganhri.org/membership/.

[44] 'De facto' independence of NHRIs is vital. *Corina Lacatus* and *Valentina Carraro*, 'National human rights institutions: independent actors in global human rights governance?' (2023) 99:3 International Affairs 1167.

[45] 'Role of national human rights institutions in facilitating access to remedy for business-related human rights abuses – Report of the Working Group on the issue of human rights and transnational corporations and other business enterprises', A/HRC/47/39/Add.3 (22 June 2021) para 39.

[46] *Asian NGO Network on National Human Rights Institutions*, On the Performance of National Human Rights Institutions in Asia (2023) 17.

'If I were to nominate the most significant contributor to the ongoing democratic backsliding of Indian democracy from 2024, it would be the fall from grace of India's electoral processes and a heavy dent in the credibility of the Election Commission of India.'[47]

Roy Chowdhury and Keane, in their book *To kill a democracy*, also highlight worries that are 'surfacing about the declining independence of governing institutions' in India, including the Election Commission.[48]

Moreover, many governments in Asia have also been targeting civil society organisations critical of government policies. Various 'legal and extra-legal methods'[49] have been employed to achieve this goal of constraining critical civil society voices, e.g., imposing stringent registration and renewal requirements, restricting foreign funding for CSOs, selective use of tax evasion or national security laws for persecution of CSOs, putting civil society leaders under surveillance and using SLAPP (strategic litigation against public participation). A Joint Analysis of FORUM-ASIA and KontraS on the Situation of Human Rights Defenders in Asia paints a grim picture: 'From 1 January 2022 to 30 June 2023, FORUM-ASIA documented 1,181 cases of violations against HRDs in 22 monitored Asian countries. A total of 2,779 HRDs–including individuals, organisations, and communities–and their family members were affected as a result.'[50]

IV. Constitutionalism on the streets

Due to various reasons (including limited institutional space for raising discontent or dissent with government policies), one could see a trend of people coming out in large numbers on streets across Asia. This may be termed as 'constitutionalism on the streets', because such mass protests have often been held to defend various constitutional values such as human rights and freedoms, democracy, equality and participation in decision making. Mass protests in recent years, for example, in Bangladesh, Hong Kong, India, Indonesia, Myanmar, Pakistan, Sri Lanka, South Korea and Thailand could be analysed from this perspective.

There are certain common features of such mass protests. First, most protests start with a relatively minor constitutional issue but then expand to cover a range of distinct but related issues or evolve to focus on wider underpinning constitutional concerns. For example, the July 2024 protests in Bangladesh started with demands from university students to abolish quotas in civil service jobs.[51] Simi-

---

[47] *Anmol Jain*, 'Democracy and the Election Commission of India: 2024 in Review' (28 December 2024), https://verfassungsblog.de/democracy-and-the-election-commission-of-india/.

[48] *Roy Chowdhury* and *Keane*, note 13.

[49] *Jain*, note 47.

[50] *FORUM-ASIA* and *KontraS*, Joint Analysis of FORUM-ASIA and KontraS on the Situation of Human Rights Defenders in Asia (2024) 2, https://forum-asia.org/wp-content/uploads/2024/04/Joint-Analysis-HRD-Situation-Jan-June-2023-REV-1-1_compressed-1.pdf.

[51] *Anbarasan Ethirajan* and *Hannah Ritchie*, 'What sparked the protests that toppled Bangladesh's PM?' (6 August 2024), https://www.bbc.com/news/articles/cq5xye1d285o.

larly, the 2019 protests in Hong Kong started against a bill allowing criminal suspects to be extradited to mainland China under certain circumstances, but then continued even after the government had decided to withdraw the said bill.[52] However, both these mass protests later ended up demanding real democracy.

Second, such protests are usually peaceful, at least to begin with – violence is resorted to fight back against the use of disproportionate force by the police or reflect frustration with non-response from the government to legitimate demands. Even when there is violence, the targets are often government institutions or public property. Third, young people have played a key role in constitutionalism on the streets.[53] They have also shown significant resilience, innovation and adaptability to continue protests despite oppressive means used by the relevant government authorities to suppress protests. Fourth, leadership for protests has been dynamic: while a networked or diffused leadership emerged during the protests in some cases, mainstream political parties played a supporting role from the periphery in other situations. Fifth, the power of social media has been harnessed by protesters to communicate, mobilise support, build advocacy beyond borders and fight against government surveillance.

One could also see the rise of *constitutional solidarity* across borders in Asia. The 'milk tea alliance' – an alliance among protesters in Hong Kong, Myanmar and Thailand to fight against authoritarian regimes – is a case point.[54] Such alliances have proved to be a powerful tool for facilitating peer learning among protesters, mobilising public opinion beyond national borders and bypassing territorial limits on protests by authoritarian regimes. At times, such alliances have provided support to protest leaders in exile, including in seeking asylum and achieving socio-economic integration.

In terms of success, constitutionalism on the streets have had a mixed success so far in Asia. For example, mass protests in Hong Kong, Myanmar, Pakistan and Thailand have not achieved the key protest demands. At the same time, the 2024 protests in Bangladesh resulted in ousting a government which had wielded significant powers for 15 years. Similarly, the 2022 protests in Sri Lanka forced President Rajapaksa to resign and flee the country. It is though yet to be seen whether these leadership changes would lead to more systemic constitutional changes or not. Further research is required to understand the role of mass public protests and social movements – including as an example of 'folk constitution-

---

[52] 'The Hong Kong protests explained in 100 and 500 words' (28 November 2019), https://www.bbc.com/news/world-asia-china-49317695.

[53] *Amnesty International*, 'New generation of young activists lead fight against worsening repression in Asia' (30 January 2020), https://www.amnesty.org/en/latest/news/2020/01/new-generation-young-activists-lead-fight-worsening-repression-asia/.

[54] *Laignee Barron*, '"We Share the Ideals of Democracy." How the Milk Tea Alliance Is Brewing Solidarity Among Activists in Asia and Beyond' (28 October 2020), https://time.com/5904114/milk-tea-alliance/.

alism'[55] – in strengthening and/or challenging our understanding of constitutionalism.

V. Caged courts

Courts across Asia find themselves in a variety of cages[56] – from a big cage with some freedoms within boundaries set by external actors to a small cage with not much space to operate independently. While in many cases, such cages have been built by the executive and/or the legislature, there are also instances where judiciary has put itself in a self-made cage, e.g., to safeguard against further attacks, backlash or restrictions. In either case, courts in Asia generally are failing to control the power of governments, including of governments in flawed democracies. In fact, courts seem to be taking a cue from powerful governments on issues of critical constitutional importance, because in 'dominant-party or fragile democracies, courts can only take a limited range of actions before they overrun the government's "zone of tolerance"'.[57]

At times, it appears that courts are becoming a tool to legitimise the exercise of (un)constitutional powers. For example, in August 2024, Thailand's Constitutional Court ordered the dissolution of Move Forward, a Thai reformist party which had won the most seats and votes in the 2023 election but was blocked from forming a government.[58] The Court reasoned that Move Forward's goal to change royal defamation laws would amount to calling for the destruction of the constitutional monarchy. Through such decisions, courts end up becoming 'partisan tools that assist one political camp to dislodge its rivals'.[59]

This Thai case is comparable to how Hong Kong courts have generally shown deference to Hong Kong government's decisions undermining human rights after the enactment of the National Security Law.[60] Although Hong Kong courts may still operate independently in deciding corporate or commercial disputes, they would be operating within a cage in dealing with politically sensitive cases. In

[55] *Kevin J Elliott*, 'Folk Constitutionalism, or Why it Matters How Ordinary People Think about the Constitution' (2024) 36:3 Critical Review: A Journal of Politics and Society 222.

[56] The term 'caged courts' is inspired by the title of *Stanley B Lubman*'s book, Bird in a Cage: Legal Reform in China after Mao (Stanford University Press, 2000).

[57] *Po Jen Yap*, 'Courts and elections in Asia' in Po Jen Yap (ed.), Judicial review of elections in Asia (Routledge, 2016) 2.

[58] See *Jonathan Head*, 'Thai court dissolves reformist party that won election' (7 August 2024), https://www.bbc.com/news/articles/crkmdd4vevxo.

[59] See *Yap*, note 57, 1, 2.

[60] See *Deva*, note 34; *Johannes Chan*, 'Judicial Responses to the National Security Law: HKSAR V Lai Chee Ying' (2021) 51 Hong Kong Law Journal 1; *Surya Deva*, 'Putting Byrnes and Hong Kong in a time machine: Human rights in 2021 under the shadow of Beijing's National Security Law' (2021) 27:3 Australian Journal of Human Rights 467.

other words, Hong Kong courts will hesitate to take decisions, which might displease Beijing or pro-Beijing media and politicians.[61]

Even the Indian Supreme Court, which is regarded as one of the most powerful apex courts in the world,[62] has behaved like a caged court during the era of powerful executives. The Court's infamous decision in *ADM Jabalpur v Shivkant Shukla*[63] during the emergency declared by Mrs Indira Gandhi is a case in point. We can see a similar trend during the current regime of Prime Minister Modi. For example, the Court's treatment of various petitions concerning Jammu and Kashmir such as the prolonged internet shutdown, arrests of activists and journalists and the abrogation of Article 370 conferring a special autonomous status shows its hesitation to take on a powerful executive on important issues of constitutionalism. Bhatia describes different strategies adopted by the Supreme Court in such cases:

> 'A delay in deciding a continuing violation of rights, a "decision" that states the law but does not apply it (and thus allows the violation of rights to continue without actual judicial scrutiny), or a decision that outsources the issue back to the executive, for it to be a judge in its own cause.'[64]

It should be acknowledged that even the caged courts can act freely at times, especially when doing so serves the interests of the government in power or at least does not challenge its power. As noted below, several public interest litigation cases would fall into this category. By demonstrating their ability to act independently in such cases, courts will try to gain a certain amount of legitimacy.

VI. Transformative constitutionalism

As constitutions generally mark a departure from the past, they inevitably reflect changes. However, the term 'transformative constitutionalism' is used to describe constitutions that seek to transform – rather than preserve – existing political, social and economic structures.[65] Saunders notes that a transformational constitution 'is directed to broader changes, in society and the economy, as well as in the governance of the state, and may place particular responsibilities on the performance of courts.'[66] Hailbronner argues that transformative constitutions

---

[61] *Michael C Davis*, 'Beijing's Crackdown on Human Rights and the Rule of Law in Hong Kong' (2021) 16:2 Asia Policy 57, 73–74.

[62] *Stephen Gardbaum*, 'What Makes for More or Less Powerful Constitutional Courts?' (2017) 39 Duke Journal of Comparative & International Law 1, 3.

[63] AIR 1976 SC 1207.

[64] *Gautam Bhatia*, 'A Constitutionalism Without the Court' (1 August 2020), https://indconlawphil.wordpress.com/2020/08/01/iclp-turns-7-a-constitutionalism-without-the-court/.

[65] *Gaurav Mukherjee*, 'Transformative Constitutionalism' in Max Planck Encyclopedia of Comparative Constitutional Law (2023).

[66] *Cheryl Saunders*, 'Constitution Transformation' (2019) UMelbLRS 1, https://www6.austlii.edu.au/cgi-bin/viewdoc/au/journals/UMelbLRS/2019/1.html#fn14.

differ from liberal constitutions in that the former conceptualise the constitution as a comprehensive order for a more just and equal society and a tool to prompt state action to that purpose.[67]

To overcome effects of colonisation, Asian countries perhaps needed transformative constitutions. The Indian Constitution, being adopted in 1950, is often cited as an early example of a transformative constitution.[68] It is for this reason that Austin had described the Indian Constitution as 'first and foremost a social document'.[69] Similarly, Bhatia shows how the Indian Constitution was consciously meant to bring political, social and economic transformation, including by altering the relationship between individuals and the society as well.[70]

Courts tend to play a vital role in transformative constitutionalism. Such a role may either be envisaged in the original constitutional text or acquired by them in the given circumstances, even by caged courts as long as doing so does not rock the government in power. Many public interest litigation cases decided by Indian Supreme Court will fall in this category in that they tried to bring the constitutional aspirations of 'justice, liberty, equality and fraternity' closer to 'We, the people of India' – for example, the Court did so by reading multiple directive principles of state policy as implied fundamental rights within Article 21 of the Constitution (the right to life).[71] In addition, the environmental jurisprudence of apex courts of Bangladesh, India and Pakistan has been transformative.[72]

---

[67] *Michaela Hailbronner*, 'Transformative Constitutionalism: Not Only in the Global South' (2017) 65 American Journal of Comparative Law 527.

[68] Outside of Asia, the South African Constitution is often regarded as a leading example of transformative constitutions. Roux notes that: 'Like the Indian Constitution, the South African Constitution also accords a much greater role to the state in overcoming past injustices, including the legacy of colonialism.' Roux, note 12.

[69] *Austin*, note 5, 50.

[70] *Gautam Bhatia*, The Transformative Constitution: A Radical Biography in Nine Acts (HarperCollins India, 2019).

[71] See, for example, *Justice P N Bhagwati*, 'Judicial Activism and Public Interest Litigation' (1984) 23 Columbia Journal of Transnational Law 561; *Upendra Baxi*, 'Taking Suffering Seriously: Social Action Litigation in the Supreme Court of India' (1985) Third World Legal Studies 107; *Clark D Cunningham*, 'Public Interest Litigation in Indian Supreme Court: A Study in the Light of the American Experience' (1987) 29 Journal of Indian Law Institute 494; *Satyaranjan P Sathe*, Judicial Activism in India (Oxford University Press, 2002); *Surya Deva*, 'Public Interest Litigation in India: A Critical Review' (2009) 28:1 Civil Justice Quarterly 19.

[72] See *Jona Razzaque*, Public interest environmental litigation in India, Pakistan, and Bangladesh (Kluwer Law International, 2004).

C. Conclusion

This paper attempts to paint some common patterns of constitutionalism on a very big Asian canvas. These patterns are merely illustrative, rather than being able to offer a complete picture of constitutionalism in Asia.

Although Asia is complex and heterogeneous, what happens (or does not happen) in Asia matters for global constitutionalism for various reasons outlined in the introduction to this paper. More research is therefore desirable on perspectives of and from Asia – or the Global South more broadly – about constitutionalism.[73] I identify three strands of such inquiry for further research. First, how Asia has adapted Western ideas of constitutionalism to local contexts. One could, for example think of the concept of secularism or the horizontal application of constitutional rights. Second, an analysis of the South-South comparison, dialogues, peer learning and transplantation of constitutionalism. This may be especially relevant because of similar social, economic, cultural and political contexts among Global South countries.[74] Third, development of the Global South perspectives on constitutionalism as well as their suitability and export to the Global North. While the Global South has historically been studied and analysed as a recipient of the Global North constitutionalism, this need not be a one-way traffic.[75] The contribution of the Global South in terms of public interest litigation and the recognition as well as enforcement of socio-economic rights, or transformative constitutionalism generally, is a case in point.

In terms of process, it will be critical that scholars from the Global South are at the centre of such research, not merely as empirical respondents of the Global North investigators but also as scholars with agency. The workshop on 'Southern Lessons for Constitutional Law' hosted at the Humboldt-Universität Berlin in September 2024, from which this paper originated, marks a genuine attempt at facilitating such horizontal dialogue between North-South scholars.

[73] Melo and Buckhart argue that 'it would be more appropriate to comprehend the constitutionalism of the global south as a "constitutionalism *from* the global south".' *Milena P Melo* and *Thiago R Buckhart*, 'A constitutionalism "of" the Global South? Epistemological reflections on emerging constitutional trends' (2022) 14:3 Revista de Estudos Constitucionais, Hermenêutica e Teoria do Direito *(RECHTD)* 420, 421.

[74] For example, 'South Asian countries … display a remarkable degree of constitutional and legal kindship' because of 'several common elements among the region's constitutions, political structures and legal systems.' *Sunil Khilnani*, *Vikram Raghavan* and *Arun K Thiruvengadam*, 'Introduction: Reviving South Asian Comparative Constitutionalism' in Sunil Khilnani, Vikram Raghavan and Arun K Thiruvengadam (eds.), Comparative Constitutionalism in South Asia (Oxford University Press, 2013) 1, 2.

[75] Reviewing Constitutionalism of the Global South, Gargarella notes that 'several countries in the "Global South" have been forced or motivated to develop novel and socially attractive legal practices, which tend to be less common in the "Global North," and which are worth examining (even though the specialized literature does not always take those experiences seriously).' *Roberto Gargarella*, 'Constitutionalism of the Global South by Daniel Bonilla Maldonadoed' (2017) 15:2 International Journal of Constitutional Law 571.

The Global North-Global South Dichotomy and Insights from the Global South on the Rule of Law

Selin Esen

A. Introduction

The rule of law is a complex and multifaceted concept shaped by various cultural, historical, and political factors across the world. While the traditional understanding of the rule of law has primarily emerged from Western liberal democracies, the experiences and perspectives of the Global South offer valuable insights that can enhance our understanding of this concept and open up new horizons to find solutions to some specific issues.[1] Below, I will first briefly discuss the distinction between the Global North and the South and the concept of the rule of law and its basic features. Finally, I will discuss some aspects of the rule of law in the Global South.

B. Understanding the Global North-Global South Dichotomy

The "global south" or "the south" has for some time been the preferred term for what used to be called the "third world" and "periphery" to categorize the non-industrialized, largely agricultural, generally low-income nations of the world which, for the most part, have at one time been colonized by the industrialized and wealthy countries of the "North". The "Global South" denotes the concept of the "third world" introduced by Alfred Sauvy in 1952 to designate nations that chose not to align with either the Western democratic first world or the communist second world.[2] While the "Global North" amounts to prosperous and industrialized states, the "Global South" refers to developing or economically disadvantaged countries. The distribution of economic and political power between rich and poor nations is highly unequal.[3] Almost all the populations in the South are also multiethnic and multicultural.[4] This dichotomy separated the "other"

[1] *Todd J. Zywicki* (2003). The Rule of Law, Freedom and Prosperity. Supreme Court Economic Review 10: 1–26.

[2] *Jacqueline Anne Braveboy-Wagner* (2009). Institutions of the Global South. Routledge: 2.

[3] *Barbara P. Thomas-Slayter* (2003). Southern Exposure. International Development and the Global South in the Twenty-First Century. Kumarian Press: 9–11.

[4] *Jacqueline Anne Braveboy-Wagner* (1986). Interpreting the Third World: Politics, Economics, and Social Issues. Praeger.

nations from the prosperous Western countries whose cultures and traditions mostly take root from Christianity.

However, there is no homogeneity within the Global South. It is inaccurate to "lump" all countries categorized as part of the Global South, often perceived as impoverished or subjected to colonialism in one box. Economically, demographically, and historically, they exhibit notable differences. Likewise, the levels of external dependence experienced by countries within the Global South vary widely.[5] Economic and cultural diversity is not exclusive to the Global South; it also extends to nations in the "Global North". For instance, the economic and cultural differences between countries such as Japan and Greece or South Korea and Romania, illustrate this point. Moreover, the West-East divide regarding democracy and the rule of law within the European Union further underscores these distinctions. Such economic and cultural variations can also exist within individual countries classified as part of the Global South or the Global North.[6]

There are numerous theories regarding the classification of countries within the Global South and the Global North. The United Nations' Finance Center for South-South Cooperation maintains arguably the world's most reputable and reliable list of countries categorized as part of the Global South. As of early 2022, the list includes 78 countries, collectively referred to as the "Group of 77 and China."[7] This classification encompasses nations from Africa, Latin America, Asia, and Oceania, including prominent examples such as South Africa, Egypt, Chile, Brazil, Colombia, Argentina, Uruguay, Mexico, China, India, Kazakhstan, Turkmenistan, Uzbekistan, Kuwait, Qatar, and North Korea. Conversely, countries such as Türkiye, Azerbaijan, Kyrgyzstan, Israel, Moldova, Georgia, Armenia, Tuvalu, Serbia, Bosnia and Herzegovina, Albania, Kosovo, and North Macedonia are not included in the scope of the Global South. Indeed, several of these countries can be seen as straddling the boundary between the 'North' and 'South' within the context of international development.[8]

The homogenizing effect of globalization on cultures and societies has become more evident, especially since the second half of the 20th century. This shift, alongside industrial breakthroughs in several »Global South« countries and the emergence of BRIC (Brazil, Russia, India, China), and its increasing influence in world politics has complicated the traditional North-South dichotomy. While

[5] *Thomas-Slayter* (2003) (n. 3): 7–8.

[6] For example, since unification, the paradox of "two Italys" of the economically underdeveloped, culturally diverse South and the industrialized and "Western" North in Italy has been analyzed from various perspectives by numerous Italian scholars. See *Antonio Gramsci* (1978). Some Aspects of the Southern Question. Selections from Political Writings 1921–1926. Lawrence and Wishart.

[7] http://www.fc-ssc.org/en/partnership_program/south_south_countries. All web links cited in this work were last accessed on 11.04.2025.

[8] *Sebastian Haug* (2021). A Thirdspace approach to the 'Global South': insights from the margins of a popular category. Third World Quarterly 42(9): 2018–2038.

the terms still evoke a context rooted in historical colonialism, neo-imperialism, and varying economic and social dynamics, they also highlight the persistent inequalities in living standards and access to resources. The term "Global South" marks a shift from in focus from mere developmental or cultural differences to a broader emphasis on geopolitical power relations, reflecting the complexities that characterize the current global landscape.[9]

C. Global South and the Rule of Law

I. The Concept of Rule of Law

There is no single definition of the rule of law. The most commonly cited distinction lies between the procedural/formal rule of law and the substantive rule of law. The formal understanding of the rule of law emphasizes that laws shoul be general, clear, and reasonably stable, certain, prospective rather than retrospective, consistent, and uniformly applied to everyone. It further stipulates that laws should not demand impossible conduct from individuals and that governmental actions be subject to judicial review.[10] This procedural perspective is often labeled as a »thin« understanding of the rule of law. Thicker conceptualizations of the rule of law encompass not only these prerequisites but also necessitate adherence to fairness-oriented institutional, economic, cultural, and political criteria.[11] This broader view incorporates substantive norms and goals, including a democratic form of government, participation, deliberation, and individual rights.

As Brian Tamanaha suggests, this dichotomy between "thin" and "thick" is not clear and can better be understood as a progression along which both formal and substantive aspects of the rule of law can be "thinner" or "thicker".[12] For example, where formal law manifests as "rule-by-law", it reflects a thin version of formal rule of law , which suggests that legal norms primarily serve to articulate and reinforce state power. In such cases, those who possess the authority to create and enforce laws do so primarily to regulate and control the populace, often lacking accountability themselves, as they evade the very rules they impose on others.[13] When formal law also embodies the principles of democracy and legal-

---

[9] *Nour Dados* and *Raewyn Connell* (2012). The Global South. Contexts. Sage Journals 11(1): 12–13.

[10] *Yasuo Hasebe* and *Cesare Pinelli* (2015). Constitutions. Routledge Handbook of Constitutional Law. (eds. Mark Tushnet, Thomas Fleiner, and Cheryl Saunders): 52.

[11] *Robin L. West* (2003). Re-Imagining Justice: Progressive Interpretations of Formal Equality, Rights, and the Rule of Law. Georgetown Public Law Research Paper No. 12–074.

[12] *Brian Z. Tamanaha* (2004). On the Rule of Law-History, Politics, Theory. Cambridge University Press: 91.

[13] *Gregory Shaffer* and *Wayne Sandholtz* (2023). The Rule of Law under Challenge: The Enmeshment of National and International Trends. Georgetown University Law Center Research Paper No. 2023/14. *Georgetown University Law Center*, https://scholarship.law.georgetown.edu/facpub/2551 https://ssrn.com/abstract=4617888: 7.

ity, the rule of law takes on a "thicker" quality. Similarly, the substantive rule of law may provide a thin version of "individual rights" or a thick version of "social welfare rights", demanding not just the recognition of rights but also the promotion of substantive equality and the safeguarding of communal well-being.

Different cultures and legal traditions define law and its place in a society differently.[14] Despite a lack of consensus on all the components of the rule of law, a set of core principles underlie the concept, which is not exclusively a Western framework. A report by the UN Secretary-General for the UN Security Council defines the rule of law as "a principle of governance in which all persons, institutions, and entities, public and private, including the State itself, are accountable to laws that are publicly promulgated, equally enforced, independently adjudicated, and which are consistent with international human rights norms and standards. It requires, as well, measures to ensure adherence to the principles of supremacy of law, equality before the law, accountability to the law, fairness in the application of the law, separation of powers, participation in decision-making, legal certainty, avoidance of arbitrariness, and procedural and legal transparency."[15] This definition indicates that, despite the differences over its precise definition and nature, there is a growing consensus about the core elements of the rule of law. This definition incorporates substantive conceptions, including consistency with "international human rights norms and standards" and "participation in decision-making".

The concept of substantive rule of law, which emphasizes social justice and equitable distribution within society, should be incorporated into the broader framework of rule of law, because there are notable disparities in the distribution of wealth and resources among social classes, ethnic and cultural communities within many countries in the South and some other countries outside the South. For this reason, legal systems that adopt the thick version of the rule of law are not exceptional for the countries in the South.

The rule of law and rule by law represent ideal-type constructs. In reality, the presence of arbitrariness exists on a spectrum, with practices diverging across a continuum. State practices vary across issue areas and among various populations. For example, Singapore operates as a "dual state", as it aligns with the 'law' of the liberal 'West' in the commercial sphere while simultaneously repressing civil and political rights.[16]

Another matter is what lessons about the rule of law we can draw from the Global South. There is a presumption that the scholarship and legal products in constitutional law, including in the field of the rule of law, produced by the

[14] *Robert L. Nelson* and *Lee Cabatingan* (2010). A Preface and an Introduction. Global Perspectives on the Rule of Law. (eds. James J. Heckman, Robert L. Nelson, and Lee Cabatingan). Routledge: 35.

[15] Report of the Secretary-General on The rule of law and transitional justice in conflict and post-conflict societies, S/2004/616, 23.8.2004: 4.

[16] *Shaffer* and *Sandholtz* (2023) (n. 13): 8.

Global South occupy a low level. While legal scholars and institutions in the North generate a majority of original academic works, those in the South provide only works that are derived from other sources. However, observe that a significant portion of the contributions from the Global North originates from only a few of countries, such as the USA, Canada, the UK, and Germany. The contributions of countries from the Global South to the rule of law are often characterized by their negative experiences and practices in this field. It is observed that, similar to the "South", academic studies on the rule of law in many countries in the "North" are generally based on an explanation of the negative experiences in these countries.

The universities and scholars in the Global South have increasingly become crucial players in advancing innovative research projects and legal publications.[17] Academic studies from the Global South on the relationship between rights and duties in various African and Asian nations make significant contributions to comprehending and explaining different traditions of the rule of law. Moreover, the creative solutions proposed by various constitutional/supreme courts in these regions to implement the rule of law significantly enrich the field. Therefore, it can be argued that the historically perceived disparity between the North and the South concerning knowledge production and stimulating experiences in the rule of law is beginning to erode.

II. Main Features of the Rule of Law in the Global South

1. Co-existence of different legal orders and inclusion of their pre-colonial institutions and values in the legal system

The introduction of models of law and the rule of law during the colonial era has had profound and varied impacts on legal systems worldwide. European powers tended to layer their norms and forms over local law already in place, resulting in a legally pluralistic landscape.[18] Combining pre-existing legal systems in former colonies with European law has produced a mosaic of distinct legal systems. The legal and constitutional orders of the Global South exhibit more pronounced, flexible, and multifaceted responses to the state law, reflecting the complexities and diversities of their historical and cultural contexts. Informal rules, institutions, and practices gain distinct importance in understanding how law in books works in action. Citizens often turn to non-state collectives and their norms, such as religious or ethnic groups, Indigenous peoples, social movements, trade unions, or business associations. The results are diverse forms of legal pluralism and non-state justice systems, which are increasingly recognized by

[17] *Daniel Bonilla Maldonado* (2013). Introduction. Constitutionalism of Global South (ed. Daniel Bonilla Maldonado). Cambridge University Press: 12–18.

[18] *Sally Engle Merry* (1988). Legal pluralism. Law & Society Review 22(5): 869–896.

constitutions across the South. One example is personal laws in India and another is self-governed Indigenous territories in Bolivia.[19]

Legal plurality in the nineteenth century became the case in some borderline countries between the North and South that were not colonized, such as the Ottoman Empire, but for different reasons. Sources of law in the empire were Islamic and customary law, and non-Muslim communities had jurisdictional power in the field of family law under the "*millet system*".[20] The first significant codification movement occurred in the second half of the nineteenth and early twentieth centuries. The goal of these reforms was to strengthen the collapsing empire by adopting European laws. The main characteristic of these laws was that they were not derived from Islamic law and Ottoman customs but were inspired by European legislation. Hence, they included secular institutions and rules inconsistent with Islamic law. New tribunals, i.e., "*nizamiye courts*", were founded to settle legal issues resulting from the new laws in the 1860s alongside Sharia courts. Other European institutions, such as the Council of State and the Audit Office, were implemented in the Ottoman legal and administrative order. Accordingly, the legal system became more pluralistic along with Islamic law, new secular law, and the "*millet system*". The legal reforms of the Turkish Republic, which was founded in 1923 after the collapse of the Ottoman Empire, maintained the efforts of the Ottoman era. Beginning in 1926, the Republic underwent a second phase of legal reception from European sources to establish a secular legal framework. Therefore, while the legal reforms of the Ottoman Empire led to a divided legal system, the legal reforms of the Turkish Republic attempted to unify it under the state's legal hierarchy. New secular laws eliminated the legal duality, and the Ottoman legal system was entirely abolished. The reforms completely rested the Turkish legal system upon secular civil (Roman) law tradition.[21]

Many nations from the Global South contextualize the rule of law within their local values, traditions, and institutions. In several countries, there have been attempts to inject local cultural and religious norms from their pre-colonial legal systems into the legal systems inherited from the colonial powers. This reflects a desire to reconcile universal principles of the rule of law with local conceptions of justice and governance.

---

[19] *Philipp Dann, Michael Riegner, Maxim Bönnemann* (2020). The Southern Turn in Comparative Constitutional Law-An Introduction. The Global South and Comparative Constitutional Law (eds. Philipp Dann, Michael Riegner, and Maxim Bönnemann). Oxford University Press: 26.

[20] *Gülnihal Bozkurt* (1989). Alman- İngiliz Belgelerinin ve Siyasi Gelişmelerin Işığı Altında Gayrimüslim Osmanlı Vatandaşlarının Hukuki Durumu (1839–1914). Türk Tarih Kurumu Basımevi.

[21] *Selin Esen* (2024). The Place of the Judiciary in the 1924 Constitution of Turkey. DPCE 61(4): 3612–3614.

The concept of *Ubuntu* in South Africa and sub-Saharan cultures exemplifies an integration of diverse legal practices and philosophies, serving as a prominent illustration of how multiple legal systems can be harmoniously blended within a single post-colonial state. *Ubuntu* is an ethical perspective and way of life. Standard sub-Saharan conceptions of the "good life" cash out self-realization strictly in terms of communal, harmonious, or cohesive relationships with others. As a social principle, *Ubuntu* establishes the mutual interdependence of human beings in the community. An *Ubuntu* ethic was the core of the founding principle and process of the Truth and Reconciliation Commission that dealt with apartheid-era crimes in a largely non-retributive manner in South Africa. Also, the Constitutional Court of South Africa appealed to the value of *ubuntu* to judge the death penalty that was inconsistent with the right to life and human dignity implied in its Constitution.[22]

Likewise, the concept of the rights of nature in the 2008 Constitution of Ecuador aligns with the indigenous aspiration to live in harmony with nature, serving as a notable example of the incorporation of pre-colonial values into the legal system. Similarly, the 2017 Constitution of Thailand guarantees the rights of individuals while recognizing the importance of communal ties in Thailand. Buddhism, the dominant religion of the country, emphasizes actions based on individuals' duties toward others rather than solely on individual rights. However, these rights are advocated very much vis-à-vis the state or vested interests rather than against each other.[23]

Accordingly, local or pre-colonial ideas influence and transform the concept of the rule of law in various Global South nations. Although this is also true for some Global North countries, this trend is more prevalent in the South. For example, in New Zealand, a Global North country, indigenous rights have been acknowledged in several ways, including the preservation of Māori cultural symbols, native values, and native relationships with ancestral lands and natural resources, through various legislative acts and court rulings. In the case of *Takamore v. Clarke* (2012), the Supreme Court recognized for the first time that Māori customary law, *tikanga*, should be taken into account within the common law. Recognizing the *Whanganui River* and its surrounding areas as "an indivisible and living whole" with legal personality by law also demonstrates how Māori legal concepts and values can influence the state legal system and the rule of law.[24]

---

[22] *Paul Nnodim* and *Austin Okigbo* (2020). Justice as Fairness and Ubuntu: Conceptualizing Justice through Human Dignity. Ethical Perspectives 27(1): 69–89; *Thaddeus Metz* (2021). Ubuntu: the Good Life. Encyclopedia of Quality of Life and Well-Being Research (ed. Flomena Maggino). Springer: 1–4.

[23] Vitat Muntarbhorn (2004). The rule of law and aspects of human rights in Thailand: from conceptualization to implementation?. Asian Discourses of Rule of Law (ed. Randall Peerenboom). Routledge.

[24] *Brian Z. Tamanaha* (2021). Legal Pluralism Explained. History, Theory, Consequences. Oxford University Press: 103–104.

2. Detailed Constitutions and Broad Rights Catalogue

Until the end of World War II, the constitutions were conceived as short and brief legal documents. As Kim Lane Scheppele has noted, modern constitutions in newer or more fragile democracies tend to rely on thick constitutional texts, which specify constitutional rights and duties in considerable detail.[25] Indeed, research conducted by Adam Chilton and Mila Versteeg indicates that between 1946 and 2016, the median number of rights enshrined in national constitutions increased from 20 to 41.[26] Today, 81 % of constitutions guarantee or aim to safeguard the right to primary education,[27] and 74 % of them protect the right to health.[28] Constitutions drafted after World War II exhibit additional features, such as granting courts the power to review the constitutionality of legislative and executive acts, as well as political activities through the principle of militant democracy. Indeed, while constitutional review was nonexistent in 1781, by 2011, 83 % of the world's constitutions included provisions for it.[29] These data show there is no significant disparity in the constitutional recognition of the rights and constitutional review between the North and the South.

Although there is no significant difference between the North and the South regarding the constitutionalization of rights, the constitutions of the Global South include a more extensive and detailed list of economic and social rights. Social injustices and the inequitable distribution of resources and opportunities are compelling matters in many countries in the South. This fact explains the role and importance of economic and social rights in tackling challenges of poverty, inequality, and marginalization that impact a significant portion of the population in these countries. Therefore, it is considered a necessity for the Global South nations that the state assumes duties and responsibilities in the economic and social sphere to achieve these goals. Consequently, economic and social rights and substantial equality play a significant role in how the Global South nations relate to the rule of law.

Besides economic and social rights, the South leads the way in constitutionalizing emerging rights. Many constitutions in the Global South provide pro-

---

[25] *Kim Lane Scheppele* (2005). Democracy by Judiciary. Or why Courts can Sometimes be more Democratic than Parliaments. Rethinking the Rule of Law after Communism (eds. Adam Czarnota, Martin Krygier, and Wojciech Sadurski). Central European University Press: 25, 37–38.

[26] *Adam Chilton* and *Mila Versteeg* (2022). The Politics of Constitutional Rights. https://ssrn.com/abstract=4097074 or http://dx.doi.org/10.2139/ssrn.4097074.

[27] *Jody Heymann*, *Amy Raub* and *Adele Cassola* (2014). Constitutional rights to education and their relationship to national policy and school enrolment. International Journal of Educational Development 39: 135.

[28] Fact sheet of the World Policy Analysis Center (2020). Constitutional Approaches to the Right to Health – World Policy Analysis Center (worldpolicycenter.org).

[29] *Tom Ginsburg* and *Mila Versteeg* (2014). Why Do Countries Adopt Constitutional Review?. *The Journal of Law, Economics, and Organization* (30): 590.

visions on minority rights, environmental rights, and nature.[30] Globally, constitutional protections for LGBT+ rights remain rare. Only five national constitutions explicitly guarantee equal rights based on sexual orientation *and* gender identity. Three of them, namely Bolivia, Ecuador, and Fiji, are located in the Global South. Also, five constitutions, including Mexico and South Africa, provide protections solely based on sexual orientation.[31] The South African Constitution is the first in the world to unequivocally recognize LGBTI+ rights by prohibiting discrimination based on sexual orientation.

Regarding emerging rights, Chile became the first country in the World to *amend its Constitution* to address the challenges of neuro-technologies, namely to protect mental data and mental integrity about the advancement of neuro-technologies; and seeks to cover different areas of brain intervention, whether for health reasons or of any other nature, through the right to mental privacy, physical integrity, decision-making capacity, equality in the face of neuro-technologies and protection against ideological biases in 2021.[32] The Chilean constitutional amendment has had an impact on other countries in the region, such as Brazil and Mexico. For instance, a constitutional amendment bill introduced in Brazil in June 2023 seeks to include protections for mental integrity and algorithmic transparency. Additionally, as of March 2024, two pending neuroprivacy bills aim to amend Mexico's Constitution.[33]

Moreover, environmental rights enjoy constitutional protection in many Global South nations. Of the more than 75 countries that include a substantive environmental right in their constitutions, only three are from the Global North, namely Belgium, Norway, and France which incorporates its Charter of the Environment. It is noteworthy that almost all the countries with substantive constitutional environmental rights are from the Global South.[34] It can be argued

[30] For example, most Latin American countries already recognize broad environmental rights in their constitutions. See *Maria Antonia Tigre*, *Natalia Urzola*, and *Alexandra Goodman* (2023). Climate litigation in Latin America: is the region quietly leading a revolution?. Journal of Human Rights and the Environment 14(1): 69.

[31] *UCLA Newsroom* (2016). LGBT rights and protections are scarce in constitutions around the World, UCLA study finds. https://newsroom.ucla.edu/releases/lgbt-rights-and-protections-are-scarce-in-constitutions-around-the-world-ucla-study-finds.

[32] *Enrique Siqueiros Fernández* and *Héctor Velázquez Fernández* (2022). Neuro-Rights and Ethical Ecosystem: The Chilean Legislation Attempt. Protecting the Mind. Challenges in Law, Neuroprotection and Neurorights (eds. Pablo López-Silva and Luca Valera). Springer: 132; *Allan McCay* (2024). Neurorights: the Chilean constitutional change. AI & Soc 39: 797–798. https://doi.org/10.1007/s00146-022-01396-0. The provision states that "the law shall regulate the requirements, conditions, and restrictions for [neurodata], and shall especially protect brain activity, as well as the information derived from it." Furthermore, scientific and technological developments are to be conducted with "respect for […] physical and mental integrity".

[33] *Beth Do, Maria Badillo, Randy Cantz, and Jameson Spivack (2024). Privacy and the Rise of "Neurorights" in Latin America.* https://fpf.org/blog/privacy-and-the-rise-of-neurorights-in-latin-america/.

[34] *Jacqueline Peel* and *Jolene Lin* (2019). Transnational Climate Litigation: The Contribution of the Global South. American Journal of International Law 113(4): 713.

that there are various reasons. First of all, these constitutions are newer. Nations from the South encounter negative consequences of environmental deterioration. Multinational companies have negative effects on the environment in these countries and transnational constitutional developments on environmental rights impact these nations.[35] Besides, some Global South countries, e.g., India, Bangladesh, Pakistan, and Nepal, that do not explicitly recognize environmental rights in their constitutions have constitutionalized these rights through judicial decisions.

Ecuador became the first country in the World to recognize the rights of nature at the constitutional level. While all legal systems define nature as property and natural resources as intended for human use and exploitation, the Ecuadorian Constitution suggests that hundreds of years of conventional legal, judicial, and political wisdom need to be reconsidered.[36] The preamble of the 2008 Constitution states that "We women and men, the sovereign people of Ecuador . . . celebrating nature, the Pachamama (Mother Earth), of which we are a part and which is vital to our existence . . . hereby decide to build a new form of public coexistence, in diversity and in harmony with nature, to achieve a good way of living, the Sumak Kawsay." Article 71 of the Constitution stipulates that nature has the right to its existence and the maintenance and regeneration of its vital cycles. In addition, Article 72 provides that nature has the right to be restored. Article 10 stipulates that nature will be subject to those rights recognized by the Constitution. The rights of nature provisions in Ecuador's Constitution, according to the Constitutional Court, are an important innovation, "rupturing the traditional paradigm of considering nature a mere object of law, to consider it as a subject like a living person."[37] These provisions reflect a game-changing cultural and legal shift from an anthropocentric view of the world to an ecocentric perspective that reflects the interdependence of all species and the ecosystems that make life on Earth possible.[38]

The second country in the world that has embraced the rights of nature is Bolivia. The Constitution of 2009 does not explicitly recognize nature or Mother Earth, "*Pachamama*", as a subject of rights. However, it states the notion of "*Buen Vivir*" (good living). Still, in 2010, Bolivia recognized the rights of *Pachamama* with Law No. 071 on Mother Earth Rights (*Ley de Derechos de la Madre Tierra*).[39] Article 5 provides that Mother Earth adopts the form of a collective

---

[35] *Sumudu Atapattu* and *Andrea Schapper* (2019). Human Rights and the Environment Key Issues. Routledge: 159.

[36] *David R. Boyd* (2017). The Rights of Nature: A Legal Revolution That Could Save the World. ECW Press: 253.

[37] *Boyd* (2017) (n. 36): 252.

[38] *Boyd* (2017) (n. 36): 242.

[39] Law No. 300 of 2012 on Mother Earth and Integral Development for Living Well (*Ley Marco de la Madre Tierra y Desarrollo Integral para Vivir Bien*) sets out provisions to protect the rights of nature. For criticism of the laws see Lorna Muñoz (2023). Bolivia's Mother Earth Laws are the Ecocentric Legislation Misleading?. ReVista. https://revista.drclas.harvard.edu/

entity of public interest. The rights of nature are recognized in other parts of the World as well. For example, Uganda recently granted the rights of nature nationally in the National Environment Act of 2019 and is the first country in Africa to recognize the legal rights of nature.[40]

The worldview of the indigenous peoples shares many elements with other indigenous cultures, such as the Māori in New Zealand, particularly in terms of the human relationship with nature. Even though the procedure of the recognition of the Māori's relationship with the natural environment in legislation and court judgments started before, New Zealand recognized the *Whanganui River's* legal personality in a treaty settlement in 2011. A law enacted in 2014 has transformed the *Urewera National Park* from a region of government-owned property to a legal entity that has the rights of a person, owns itself, and must be managed in a way that respects its rights.[41]

Another concept on the rise is that of future generations. The rights or interests of future generations, and the rights of nature in a theoretical context were put forward and developed by the legal scholars from the Global North starting in the 1970s.[42] However, the Global South has led their constitutionalization.[43] For example, the Constitution of Argentina refers to future generations as well as human development, stating, "All residents enjoy the right to a healthy, balanced environment that is fit for human development and by which productive activities satisfy current necessities without compromising those of future generations" (Article 41). Similarly, the Bolivian Constitution cites both present and future generations and takes it one step further by according rights to other living things (Article 33). The Ecuadorian, Kenyan, and South African constitutions are other examples from the South that contain provisions for future generations.

---

bolivias-mother-earth-laws-is-the-ecocentric-legislation-misleading/; *Luis A. López Zamora* (2023). The Recognition of the Rights of Nature in Latin America –The Lost Linkage with the Rights of Future Generations. Representing the Absent (eds. Hélène Ruiz Fabri, Valérie Rosoux, and Alessandra Donati). Nomos: 478–480.

[40] *Boyd* (2017) (n. 36): 242.

[41] *Boyd* (2017) (n. 36): 242.

[42] *Yumiko Nakanishi* (2023). The Rights of and Obligations towards Future Generations. Representing the Absent (eds. Hélène Ruiz Fabri, Valérie Rosoux, and Alessandra Donati). Nomos: 237. Christopher Stone first claimed in the 1970s that "nature itself should have legal rights". Stone argued that technically there is no legal barrier to granting rights to nature, given that other non-human entities such as ships and corporations have legal rights conferred upon them. It should be given legal rights to forests, oceans, rivers, and other so-called 'natural objects' in the environment–indeed, to the natural environment as a whole. *Christopher D. Stone* (1972). Should Trees Have Standing? Law, Morality and the Environment. Southern California Law Review 45: 450.

[43] Note that the 1946 Japanese Constitution is one of the few examples in the Global North in the 20th century that recognizes the rights of future generations. Article 11 states that "[the] fundamental human rights guaranteed to the people by this Constitution shall be conferred upon the people of this and future generations as eternal and inviolate rights." *Nakanishi* (2023) (n. 42): 241.

Today, the rights of future generations are on the rise both in the constitutions of the North and South.[44]

Note that some of the constitutions of the South incorporate rights that are not explicitly recognized by reference to all the rights in certain human rights conventions. The most notable example is Argentina. When Argentina amended its constitution in 1994, it incorporated ten human rights treaties and conventions, granting them the status of constitutional law (Art 75.22). There are other examples from the South, namely the Tanzanian Constitution incorporates the Universal Declaration of Human Rights (Art. 9). The constitutions of Burundi, Madagascar, and Mauritania refer to the African Charter on Human and Peoples' Rights.

The rights may also be recognized or expanded through judicial rulings. Several courts in the Global South are particularly proactive in recognizing the rights. For example, the Indian Supreme Court created a new category of social rights that had previously not been recognized in the Indian Constitution. The court understood that many of the Constitution's civil-political rights would become meaningless if they weren't supported by certain economic and social measures that guarantee the effective exercise of these rights.[45] Some of the most notable examples involve the right to life as outlined in Article 21 of the Constitution, which states that "no person shall be deprived of their life or personal liberty except according to the procedure established by law". The court understood Article 21 to imply the rights to livelihood, health, free and compulsory education up to the age of 14 years, shelter, an unpolluted environment, clean drinking water, privacy, legal aid, and speedy trial. Additionally, this provision has been innovatively applied to address violations of the right to life and personal liberty committed by non-state actors, allowing for the possibility of compensation for infringements of the fundamental rights.[46]

In 2011, an Ecuadorian court recognized the rights of a river to flow, to perform essential functions, and to be free from pollution.[47] The Colombian Constitutional Court in 2016 recognized nature's rrpersonhood by granting legal rights to the *Atrato River*.[48] Moreover, the Supreme Court of Justice of Colombia recognized the Colombian Amazon's legal rights in 2018 and the *Isla de Salamanca National Park* in 2020. The Indian High Court recognized the rights of the

[44] *Renan Araujo* and *Leonie Koessler* (2022). The Rise of the Constitutional Protection of the Future Generations. Verfassungsblog, https://verfassungsblog.de/the-rise-of-the-constitutional-protection-of-future-generations/.

[45] *Michaela Hailbronner* (2017). Transformative Constitutionalism: Not Only in the Global South. The American Journal of Comparative Law 65: 547.

[46] *Surya Deva* (2013). The Rule of Law in India: The Chasm between Paper and Practice. The Rule of Law: Comparative Perspective (eds. Guiguo Wang and Fan Yang). City University Hong Kong Press: 39.

[47] *Tigre*, *Urzola*, and *Goodman* (2023) (n. 30): 87.

[48] T622/16 Nov. 10, 2016.

Ganges and *Yamuna* rivers in 2017.[49] The Islamabad High Court recognized the legal personhood of an elephant, ruling that it possesses constitutional protection to dignity.[50]

The Supreme Court of the Philippines, in the case of *Minors Oposa*,[51] emphasized that ecological intergenerational justice needs to be established based on the right to a balanced and healthy environment. The court asserted that it is the duty of each generation to protect the rights of future generations with the aim of maintaining the rhythm and harmony of nature. As such, the present generation has the right to stand on behalf of future generations. This decision has paved the way to a set of procedural rules that led "any Filipino citizen in representation of others, including … generations yet unborn". With this ruling, the court has expanded ratione personae of ecological rights to minors and nature. Likewise, the Colombian courts have made relevant rulings.[52] In the case of the *Atrato River*, the Constitutional Court of Colombia underlined the importance of protecting the biological and cultural diversity of the nation for future generations.[53] In the case of *Future Generations v the Ministry of the Environment and Others* in 2018, the Supreme Court of Colombia recognized the rights of future generations regarding the environment, concluding that the government's inaction on climate change and deforestation violated the youth's rights. This landmark case opened the door to youth climate lawsuits by substantially expanding constitutional provisions to future generations in the region.[54] Indeed, taking this ruling as an example, a group of young people filed a lawsuit, i.e. *Álvarez et al v. Peru* with similar demands in 2019 in Peru. The case remains pending.

The 1991 Constitution of Colombia recognizes the right to prior consultation. Article 330 of the Constitution indicates that cultural minorities in Colombia have the right to determine which moral, political, and legal norms are to regulate their territory, how to use the natural resources in their territory, and who may settle on and move across their lands, and to demand that their authorities be consulted on any project or piece of legislation that affects them directly.[55]

---

[49] *Mohd. Salim v. State of Uttarakhand & others* (2017). High Court of Uttarakhand at Nainital.

[50] *James R. May* (2021). The case for environmental human rights: recognition, implementation, and outcomes. Cardozo Law Review 42(3): 1010–1011. On the other hand, the Supreme Court of the Philippines in a case in 2015, ruled that it was unnecessary to give marine mammals legal standing because Filipino rules allow any citizen, as a steward of nature, to bring a lawsuit to enforce that country's environmental laws. In general, courts still prefer to grant standing to humans rather than nature, but that may be on the brink of changing. *Boyd* (2017): 165–166.

[51] Supreme Court of the Philippines, *Minors Oposa v. Secretary of the Department of Environment and Natural Resources* (DENR) 33 ILM 173, 177, 185 (1994).

[52] See the case of the Colombian Amazon of the Supreme Court of Justice.

[53] T-622/16, 2016.

[54] *Tigre*, *Urzola*, and *Goodman* (2023) (n. 30): 89–90.

[55] Note that the right to prior consultation of indigenous peoples was recognized by law in

The Constitutional Court of Colombia has developed case law regarding prior consultation and created a set of participation rights derived from the ILO Convention No. 169 of 1989, which concerns Indigenous and Tribal Peoples in Independent Countries, which Colombia ratified in 1991, as well as relevant provisions within the Colombian Constitution. Consequently, the Court has rendered the right to prior consultation a fundamental right.[56] It broadened the scope of the right finding that it includes the right for minorities to veto government decisions that threaten their existence as distinct cultures or impose undue and excessive burden on them.[57] Accordingly, the Court also broadened the communities entitled to this right and established who is obligated to conduct proceedings, the procedures to be followed, and the legal effects that arise from non-compliance with the process.[58] Rulings of the Constitutional Court have made noteworthy contributions to the instructions, application standards, and criteria for the application of prior consultation in matters related to the international treaty.

Several countries in the Global South have also recognized the right to prior consultation through judicial decisions. The Mexican Supreme Court, for example, has issued multiple rulings in recent years affirming this right. In 2015, the Court reversed an administrative decision granting a license for Monsanto to undertake large-scale plantings of genetically modified soy on the Yucatan Peninsula and other areas of the country, holding that the required prior consultation had not been carried out.[59]

Peru. *Kantuta Vallenas*, *Lucila Pautrat*, and *Catty Samaniego* (2010). Analisis de la ley consulta previa a los pueblos indigenas, y criterios para su implementacion en el contexto del debate del proyecto de ley forestal y de fauna silvestre. Sociedad Peruana de Ecodesorollo. Lima: 21–22.

[56] Decision of SU-039 of 1997; Decision of SU-383 of 2003. *Manuel Jose Cepada Espinosa* and *David Landau* (2017). Colombian Constitutional Law Leading Cases. Oxford University Press: 258 and 260.

[57] Decision of T-769/09 of 2009; Decision of T-129/11 of 2011. *Daniel Bonilla Moldonado* (2013). Self Government and Cultural Identity: The Colombian Constitutional Court and the Right of Cultural Minorities to Prior Consultation. Constitutionalism of the Global South The Activist Tribunal of India, South Africa, and Colombia (ed. Daniel Bonilla Maldonado). Cambridge University Press: 270–272.

[58] *Bonilla Moldonado* (2013) (n. 57): 276. Also in the case of *Future Generations v. Ministry of Environment and Others*, the Supreme Court of Columbia provided the remedy to the youth plaintiffs including their participation in developing a plan for Amazon conservation. https://climatecasechart.com/non-us-case/future-generation-v-ministry-environment-others/.

[59] N. 195/15 of 2015. *Cepada Espinosa* and *Landau* (2017) (n. 56): 270.

D. Constitutional review

The rule of law requires judicial review of legislative and administrative actions. Although the concept of judicial review of executive actions has been well established, judicial review of laws became widespread only after World War II. Today, 158 out of 191 constitutions include provisions for constitutional review. Recognition of the constitutional review often coincides with the introduction of constitutions with a broad list of rights. Constitutional review is closely associated with the protection of rights in both in the Global North and the Global South.[60]

Some courts have emerged as major forces in strengthening or implementing the rule of law, including the German, Italian, Spanish, and Portuguese constitutional courts in the Global North, as well as the Indian, South African, and Colombian constitutional courts in the Global South. Notable precedents on certain matters, such as the state of emergency, have also been established by various courts, including the Turkish Constitutional Court and the Portuguese Constitutional Court. Among others, the Philippine and Pakistani courts have taken an active stance on environmental matters. Constitutionalism in the Global South is characterized by active high court oversight of the fundamental elements of the constitutional structure, referred to variously as the "protection of the basic structure" in India and Kenya, or the prohibition of the "substitution of the constitution" in Colombia.

The Supreme Court of Chile became the first court to rule on neuro-technologies in 2023, following the inclusion of related provision in its constitution. The plaintiff alleged that his brain data was insufficiently protected by the US-based Emotiv's "insight" device, a headband that records detailed information about the brain's electrical activity. Ultimately, the Court found that Emotiv violated the plaintiff's constitutional rights to physical and psychological integrity as well as the right to privacy, dismissing Emotiv's claims that the harm was hypothetical. Citing both Chilean domestic law and international human rights law, the court emphasized that Emotiv retained the plaintiff's data for research purposes, even in anonymized form, without obtaining prior consent for this specific purpose. This judgment establishes a precedent for neuro privacy litigation.[61]

---

[60] *Tom Gingsburg* (2008). "The Global Spread of Constitutional Review". The Oxford Handbook of Law and Politics (eds. Keith E. Whittington, R. Daniel Kelemen, and Gregory A. Caldeira). Oxford University Press: 82–85.

[61] *Do, Badillo, Cantz, and Spivack (2024) (n. 33).*

E. Judicial Activism on Certain Matters

Judicial activism concerning certain matters, such as socioeconomic rights, access to justice, indigenous rights, and state of emergency is particularly noteworthy in discussions about the rule of law. An edited volume by Daniel Bonilla suggests that the constitutionalism of the Global South depends partly on a unique set of topics important to those countries. While some issues, such as the challenges faced by vulnerable and marginalized groups in accessing justice, may have special emphasis in the Global South countries, they are not exclusive to the region.

Nevertheless, the challenges are likely to be considerably greater in developing contexts than in wealthier and more mature democracies. Courts in the South may need to be more creative in their remedies to address the capacity deficiencies exhibited by branches of the executive. In this way, judges in several countries of the Global South have redefined the term "activist Bench," by reinterpreting the nature and characteristics of judicial power and its enforceability. For example, consider the Supreme Court of India. Although the Indian Constitution does not explicitly guarantee due process, the Supreme Court introduced this principle through judicial interpretation.[62] Furthermore, by a joint reading of articles 14 and 21 of the Constitution that guarantee equality before the law and the right to life, courts in India have developed a substantive model of the rule of law, concluding any law or executive action that is not 'just, fair and reasonable' can be declared unconstitutional.[63]

The "unconstitutional state of affairs" (*estado de cosas inconstitucional*) doctrine, developed by the Colombian Constitutional Court, exemplifies the creative solutions developed by the judiciary in the Global South to accomplish the rule of law. This doctrine provides a legal mechanism through which a court orders competent authorities to take necessary actions to rectify factual circumstances that clearly contradict the constitution. These actions must fall within the authorities' responsibilities and be carried out within a reasonable timeframe. The Colombian Constitutional Court deems its intervention in public policy as exceptional in a state governed by the rule of law that guarantees the separation of powers. When the court issues an order, its work regarding the case does not end with the judgment. The court supervises and monitors the compliance of the orders by the administration to ensure that progress is made toward the full protection of the constitutional rights in question.[64] Since 1997, the court has invoked the "structural remedies" in various cases involving the massive and

[62] *Maneka Gandhi v Union of India*, AIR 1978 SC 97. *Deva* (2013) (n. 46): 38.

[63] *Singh*, Shukla's Constitution of India (n 21) 201–04. *Deva* (2013) (n. 46): 39.

[64] *Samuel David Martinez Castrillon* and *Luisa Fernanda Cano Blandon* (2023). El estado de cosas inconsticional y el principio de unidad de la jurisdiccion en Colombia. Estudios de Derecho 15: 18–22.

systematic violation of the fundamental rights, such as conditions of the prisoners, forced displacement due to the internal armed conflict, and environmental issues. In these cases, the Colombian Constitutional Court identified the repeated, systematic, and massive violation of rights stemming from the actions or omissions of various public institutions. These failures contributed to the deep economic crisis and social inequality, demonstrating the incoherence between the principles embodied in the legal system and their effective implementation in the social aspects of the communities.[65] Other courts in the region, such as the Brazilian Supreme Federal Court, have borrowed this doctrine from the Colombian Constitutional Court.

Note that before the Colombian Constitutional Court adopted this doctrine, the Supreme Court of India issued similar rulings from the 1980s onwards, providing structural solutions to address structural problems. In case of *Hussainara Khatoon v. State of Bihar*, the Supreme Court of India acknowledged widespread human rights violations in prisons, where inmates had served extended terms without the commencement of their trials. To expedite the release of the prisoners, the court ordered various state agencies to inspect the conditions inside the prison and submit a report. The court reviewed the same case over the span of fifteen years and issued seven separate orders throughout that period. Environmental law litigation in India has also taken on a similar form, with courts frequently issuing orders and enforcing their compliance through *ongoing mandamus*.[66]

At one extreme, we may find the Supreme Court of Argentina. The Court established the "*de facto law*" doctrine, which ascribes validity to laws enacted by regimes that came to power through a coup d'etat. Congress nullified the so-called self-amnesty law, a law that the military had enacted right at the end of their rule to cover the abuses of human rights committed under their regime in 1983. The nullification was unanimously approved by Congress, and the law was subsequently upheld by the Supreme Court, thus breaking away from the doctrine of *de facto law* for the first time in more than a century. However, in 1991, the Supreme Court resumed the old doctrine with the positivist argument that the laws enacted by Congress should be deemed valid regardless of the "affective or ideological evaluation" that could be made of military regimes.[67]

---

[65] *Juan Pablo Sarmiento Erazo*, *Luis Miguel Llorente*, and *Laura Martinez Hernandez* (2022). Conexidad prospectiva: del estado de cosas inconstitucional a los ecosistemas como sujetos de derecho-aportes desde la experiencia colombiana. Revista de Investigacoes Constitucionais 9(2): 307–311.

[66] *Kartik Kalra* (2023). Explainer: The Emerging 'Unconstitutional State of Affairs' Doctrine. https://www.jurist.org/features/2023/02/03/explainer-an-unconstitutional-state-of-affairs/.

[67] *Boaventura de Sousa Santos* (2020). Toward a New Legal Common Sense.Law, Globalization, and Emancipation. 3rd ed., Cambridge University Press: 383–384.

The constitutions and judicial case law of the Global South produce creative institutions, mechanisms, and solutions to certain issues. Below, some of the interesting regulations and mechanisms regarding the environment, justice, and emergencies in the Global South will be discussed, since an exhaustive examination of the original institutions and solutions created in these countries is beyond the scope of this study.

I. Issues on the climate crisis

The South's approach to climate litigation differs from the North's. The rights-based claims regarding climate change in the Global South are more prominent than in the Global North jurisprudence. One of the reasons for this difference may be the fact that many of the constitutions in the Global South have a broad list of rights.[68] This approach has the potential to promote social justice, aiming at protecting vulnerable populations. Cases in the Global North countries are more focused on science and economic cost-based, as they aim to reduce the negative effects of climate change.[69] Cases with a science-based framing concentrate on reducing greenhouse gas emissions to prevent dangerous interference with the climate system. In the Global North, climate litigation is used to increase the governments' determination on climate change by requesting direct regulatory action.[70] In the Global South, litigation sometimes is employed by governments to protect the ecosystem and the vulnerable populations of the nation against climate change.[71]

A significant portion of cases in the Global South countries relates to the enforcement of the existing laws. However, for example, in South Africa, courts are not only enforcing existing legislation but also establishing new goals by interpreting existing legislation to require additional climate considerations. Litigation offers a route for civil society to push for enhanced legislation and targets, and to implement existing or inferred ones. Applicants target administrative decisions and legal frameworks that augment greenhouse gas emissions associated with land-use change and carbon-intensive projects. A significant portion of

---

[68] *Peel* and *Lin* (2019): 712. For instance see *Leghari v. Pakistan* (W.P. No. 25501/2015), Lahore High Court Green Bench, Order of September 4, 2015; *Farooq v. Pakistan; Shrestha v. Prime Minister (Supreme Court of Nepal, 2018, no. 10210); Rodríguez Peña y otros v. Colombia* (Supreme Court of Justice of Colombia, 2018); *Alberto Castilla Salazar v. Colombia (*C-035/16, Constitutional Court of Colombia, 2016); *Earthlife Africa Johannesburg v. Minister of Envtl. Affairs* (High Court of South Africa 2017 (2) All SA 519 (GP)); PSB et al. v. Brazil (Federal Supreme Court of Brazil, 2022).

[69] *Peel* and *Lin* (n. 34): 722.

[70] See *Urgenda v. Government of the Netherlands* (Ministry of Infrastructure and the Environment), ECLI:NL:RBDHA:2015:7145, Rechtbank Den Haag, C/09/456689/HA ZA 13–1396; *Juliana et al. v. United States of America et al.*, F.Supp. 3d 1224, 1236 (D. Or. 2016).

[71] *Joana Setzer* and *Lisa Benjamin* (2020). Climate Litigation in the Global South: Constraints and Innovations. Transnational Environmental Law 9(1): 77–101.

these cases in Latin America concerns the role of crucial ecosystems as carbon sinks, like the Amazon region in the cases of Brazil, Colombia, Ecuador, and Peru.[72] The picture in India looks different, with courts issuing orders to existing non-climate-specific regulations in tourism and transportation, combined with general environmental constitutional provisions, to ensure more climate-friendly outcomes. Also in Pakistan, dynamic judicial and legislative interactions illustrate new opportunities for advancing climate action in highly vulnerable countries.[73]

On the other hand, litigation brought against governments advocating for new or improved laws is also a significant trend in the Global North.[74] Note that the rights-based litigation has been on the rise globally following the adoption of the Paris Agreement in 2015. The cases of *Urgenda* before the Dutch Supreme Court in 2015 and Neubauer before the German Constitutional Court in 2021 exemplify this trend.

II. Access to Justice

In many countries in the Global South, marginalized communities face barriers to accessing legal remedies due to factors such as geographic constraints, economic disparities, and social inequalities. Accordingly, access to justice for disadvantaged groups remains an important issue for many countries in the Global South. One of the distinctive elements of the South is the emergence of alternative and partly collectivized channels and instruments to use the law, but also to resist the law and the state. These avenues can often be found under "access to justice". In the context of poverty and inequality, access to justice is facilitated by innovative procedural mechanisms that "bring justice within reach of the poor masses".[75]

Constitutions throughout the Global South provide for expedited legal procedures. For example, the greater procedural accessibility of Latin American constitutional justice to society is well beyond what we find in the USA or Europe. These procedures are known as the "*amparo*", "*writ of protection*", or "*tutela*" in Latin America,[76] "*public interest litigation*" in India, or "*Writ of Kalikasan*" in the Philippines. Indeed, in contrast to the amparos of Germany, Spain, or Türkiye, most Latin American writs can be used to challenge laws or even treaties, not only state actions and administrative regulations, as well as the conducts of private actors. Accordingly, countries like Colombia, Ecuador, El

---

[72] *Juan Auz* (2022). Human Rights-Based Climate Litigation: A Latin American Cartography. Journal of Human Rights and the Environment 13(1): 114–136.

[73] *Setzer* and *Benjamin* (n. 71): 6–60.

[74] *Peel* and *Lin* (n. 34): 714–715.

[75] *People's Union for Democratic Rights v. Union of India*. 1982 AIR 1473.

[76] *Allan R. Brewer-Carías* (2008). Constitutional Protection of Human Rights in Latin America: A Comparative Study of Amparo Proceedings. Cambridge University Press.

Salvador, Bolivia, and Guatemala have set up mechanisms for public actions of unconstitutionality, which enable individuals to challenge laws and seek their annulment.[77]

In addition, constitutions across the Global South create new procedures and institutions to strengthen the rule of law. The Brazilian constitutional experience provides a notable example. The previous Brazilian constitutions, especially the 1967 Constitution drafted by the authoritarian regime, provided an extensive list of rights, including social rights. However, these provisions were often unimplemented through judicial review. Courts argued that laws needed to be enacted by Congress and the President, since they were not self-applicable. Consequently, in many cases, the legislature refrained from passing laws in areas concerning constitutional rights, resulting in these rights having little practical impact. Ultimately, "*Mandado de Injunção*" was introduced to the 1988 Constitution to address legislative omissions. Article 5.LXXI of the Constitution stipulates that, such an injunction »shall be granted whenever the absence of a regulatory provision impairs the exercise of constitutional rights and liberties, as well as the prerogatives inherent to nationality, sovereignty, and citizenship«. This procedural innovation was recognized as a ground-breaking mechanism for expediting the implementation of the constitution.[78] Various judicial tools, such as "*vía de hecho*" in Colombia and "*arbitrariedad*" in Argentina, allow high courts to correct exercises of judicial adjudication on constitutional grounds beyond the options available under standard procedures.[79]

Some courts in the Global South have interpreted forms of legal action broadly to provide a more extensive protective umbrella for the rights. One notable example is "*Public interest litigation*" (PIL) in India. "Public interest litigation" refers to legal actions initiated in a court of law aimed at enforcing public interest, general interest, or interests of a particular group. "Public interest litigation" also serves as a mechanism against the denial of those rights or the infliction of wrongs that are inherently diffuse, meaning that no single individual is sufficiently affected to seek remedy on their own; rather, all individuals are collectively impacted. The purpose of "public interest litigation" is not to enforce the rights of one person against another, but to extend justice to marginalized social groups. Therefore, it is less about individual benefit and more about the welfare of the collective good of a class.[80] The origins of "public interest litiga-

---

[77] *Francisca Pou Giméne* (2017). Supreme and Constitutional Courts: Directions in Constitutional Justice. Routledge Handbook of Law and Society in Latin America (eds. Rachel Sieder and Karina Ansolabehere). Routledge.

[78] *Diego Werneck Arguelhes* (2020). Transformative Constitutionalism. A View from Brazil. The Global South and Comparative Constitutional Law (eds. Philipp Dann, Michael Riegner, and Maxim Bönnemann). Oxford University Press: 175–176.

[79] *Pou Giméne* (2017) (n. 71).

[80] *Amit Baisoya* (2024). The Concept of Public Interest Litigation in India: A Dynamic Approach. Trinity Law Review 4(1): 3.

tion" can be traced to the Global North. Nevertheless, there is a significant distinction between the North and India regarding the purpose of this mechanism. While class actions or group litigation primarily aim for efficiency, "public interest litigation" in India seeks to facilitate access to the courts for ordinary citizens in order to pursue legal redress.[81]

Unlike the "public interest litigation" in the Global North countries, such as Canada and the USA, the legal aid/public interest movement in India has almost entirely been initiated and led by the judiciary.[82] This represents a significant standard of judicial creativity and sensitivity toward challenges faced by the weak and vulnerable in society. Judges are motivated to use this strategy as a means of delivering justice to the weak.[83] Consequently, "public interest litigation" has evolved into an instrument to promote the rule of law, advocate for fairness and transparency, fight corruption within the administration, and enhance the overall accountability among government agencies. The most important contribution of this mechanism has been to bring courts closer to the disadvantaged groups of society and broaden the jurisprudence of fundamental rights. "Public interest litigation's" procedural flexibility has attracted criticism, primarily due to the variability in monitoring and the potential for different cases to take diverse directions.[84] Recently, multiple countries in the Global South have incorporated the "public interest litigation" into their constitutions.[85]

The mechanism known as *amparo*, *writ of protection*, or *tutela*, is also interpreted broadly by the judiciary to facilitate access to justice for disadvantaged groups. A notable example is the Colombian Constitutional Court's ruling in the case of the *Atrato River*. The court dismissed the claim that the writ of amparo was designed to protect only collective rights (held by humans) and not fundamental rights. The court ruled that the *amparo* was suitable for protecting both collective and fundamental rights. It concluded that, given the harm constituted by both collective and fundamental rights and the uncertainties surrounding the effectiveness of alternative legal mechanisms, such as the "*popular action procedure*", the *writ of amparo* should be considered an instrument for accessing justice.[86]

Note that not all courts embrace this approach. The Turkish Constitutional Court is a noteworthy example that does not actively expand the scope of the

[81] *Deva* (n. 46): 21.

[82] *Jamie Cassels* (1989). Judicial Activism and Public Interest Litigation in India: Attempting the

Impossible?. The American Journal of Comparative Law 37(3): 497.

[83] *Baisoya* (n. 80): 2.

[84] *Anuj Bhuwania* (2017). Courting the People: Public Interest Litigation in Post-Emergency India. Cambridge University Press; Deva (n. 46).

[85] *J. Oloka-Onyango* (2017). When Courts Do Politics. Public Interest Law and Litigation in East Africa. Cambridge Scholars Publishing: 105–106.

[86] *López Zamora* (n. 39): 486.

rights. The court finds individual applications inadmissible in environmental cases if the claimant has not been directly harmed, as such claims would constitute actio popularis.[87] Accordingly, it concluded that a local association, which sought to protect the region's ecological environment , could not be considered a victim in its individual application against a decree from the council of ministers permiting a construction of a hydro-electric power plant. The court determined that the association's rights, as derived from its legal personhood had not been violated. The court disregarded the violation of the constitutional rights of the members of the association, including their rights to family, environment, and property.[88] While the general tendency in the case law of the Turkish Council of State is to construe judicial remedies as broadly as possible, the Constitutional Court's narrow approach to individual applications results in a decline in judicial protection.[89]

Another interesting example is the "*gacaca*" courts, which were revived and adapted to address genocide cases in Rwanda in 1994. The "*Gacaca*" is an indigenous dispute resolution mechanism. It means "small grass" referring to the lawns where community elders would gather to resolve conflicts both within families and among community members. The "*gacaca*" courts were initially established to expedite the prosecution of tens of thousands of individuals following the 1994 genocide in Rwanda and to involve the public in the process of transitional justice.[90] Established in 2000, these courts employed a unique structure that aimed to guarantee fair trials in innovative ways. By 2008, more than 1 million individuals were brought before these courts. The courts functioned within communities and encouraged extensive public participation, providing transparency and much greater public oversight than in traditional courts.[91] Even though it is far from a perfect model, Rwanda's experience highlights the importance of context-specific strategies and the need to adapt reforms to unique historical and social circumstances.[92]

[87] See Case of *Ayşe Sevtap Uzun*, No: 2013/6260, 13/4/2016, § 37–41.

[88] No: 2013/1212, 12/9/2013. *Muharrem İlhan Koç* and *Recep Kaplan* (eds.) (2017). Bireysel Başvuru Kabul Edilebilirlik Kriterleri Rehberi. Ankara: 130–131.

[89] *Bertil Emrah Oder* (2013). Anayasa Mahkemesi'ne Bireysel Başvuru: Başvuruculara Öneriler. Anayasa Mahkemesine Bireysel Başvuru Hakkı Panel Notları. İstanbul Barosu Yayınları: 33–34.

[90] *Timothy Longman* (2009). An Assessment of Rwanda's Gacaca Courts. Peace Review 21(3): 306.

[91] *Longman* (n. 90): 307 and 310.

[92] *Chidiogo Uzoamaka Akpuokwe*, *Adekunle Oyeyemi Adeniyi*, *Seun Solomon Bakare* and *Nkechi Emmanuella Eneh* (2024). The Impact of Judicial Reforms on Legal Systems: A Review in African Countries. International Journal of Applied Research in Social Sciences 6(3): 204.

III. Emergency regimes

The effective exercise of the rule of law during emergency regimes varies widely from country to country. The judicial review of emergency measures and decrees during emergency regimes is particularly important to ensure that the executive respects the constitutional limits. This means that emergency decrees, decree-laws, and other administrative measures must be subject to judicial control. Since the countries in the Global South experience emergency regimes more frequently than the North, their constitutions contain more detailed provisions regarding states of exception. Some of the constitutional/supreme courts also act as activists to ensure the maintenance of political power within the constitutional limits during periods of emergency.

According to the Colombian Constitution, decrees that declare a state of emergency, or issued under a state of emergency must be reviewed by the Colombian Constitutional Court and must satisfy several conditions. Furthermore, certain types of legal instruments, including emergency decrees, are automatically submitted to the court for review (Arts. 212–215). The court has established that, within the constitutional law of exception, the constitutional block is composed of the Constitution, the instruments of international humanitarian law, the treaties recognizing human rights, rights that may not be suspended during the state of exception and the statutory law governing state of exception. Indeed, Article 93 of the Colombian Constitution stipulates that provisions of international human rights treaties that cannot be limited during emergencies are directly incorporated as the highest norms of the Colombian legal order. Other provisions of international human rights treaties should be utilized in the interpretation of domestic constitutional law. Subsequently, the court examined the contents of the constitutional block, focusing on relevant provisions in the International Covenant on Civil and Political Rights (ICCPR) and the American Convention on Human Rights. The Court's long-standing case law regarding emergency regimes has emphasized that the government cannot use a state of exception to address issues that are "chronic" or "structural" in nature. Such issues should instead be addressed by the parliament through ordinary legislative processes.[93] The Colombian Constitution grants the president legislative powers and the power to issue emergency decrees with the force of law during states of exception. These decree-laws are temporary in cases of a state of internal commotion and permanent in cases of a state of economic, social, and ecological emergency, until and unless Congress decides to change or revoke them. As a result, 40 % of decrees declaring a state of emergency issued by the President have been struck down or modified by the court. Additionally, 23 of 55 emergency decree-laws were nullified or modified by the Court between 1992 and 2020.[94]

---

[93] *Cepada Espinosa* and *Landau* (n. 56): 301.

[94] *Andrea Scoseria Katz* (2020). Taming the prince: Bringing presidential emergency powers under law in Colombia. International Journal of Constitutional Law 18(4): 1201–1230.

This statistical data indicates that the court strictly monitors the executive branch during a state of emergency. Notwithstanding, in recent years, it has been suggested that Colombia is trending back in a pro-presidential direction as the Court recedes in response to mounting political pressure and criticism.

The activism of the Turkish Constitutional Court regarding emergency decree-laws is worthy of examination. The 1982 Constitution of Türkiye provides for the executive branch to issue emergency decree-laws during emergency regimes. Emergency decree-laws can limit and even suspend constitutional rights (Art. 15).[95] More importantly, unlike the Colombian Constitution, the constitutionality of emergency decree-laws in Türkiye is not subject to judicial review (Art 148). However, once ratified by the parliament, these emergency decree-laws transform into ordinary laws, which can then be reviewed by the Constitutional Court. This restriction on the Constitutional Court's jurisdiction has received considerable criticism, since some of the most egregious human rights violations occur during emergency regimes.

The Constitutional Court partly eliminated the adverse consequences of this restriction that infringes upon the principle of the rule of law with three decisions in 1991 and 2003.[96] In these cases, the Court pointed out that emergency regimes are limited 'legal regimes' deriving from the Constitution within the understanding of a 'democratic state governed by the rule of law'. According to the court the classification of a legal document designated by the parliament or the executive does not dictate its eligibility for constitutional review. In determining the legal status of a rule, the Constitutional Court considers its substantive content rather than its formal title. The Constitution grants the government the power to issue decree-laws during a state of emergency (Art 121 and 122), but it also imposes several limitations on the exercise of this power. That is to say, emergency decree-laws can only be issued during the time of emergency, on matters necessitated by the emergency, and they prevail only in the regions where the emergency regime has been declared. Accordingly, the court considered an 'emergency decree-law' as an 'ordinary decree law' if it exceeded the limits drawn by articles 121 and 122 of the Constitution and reviewed its constitutionality.

---

[95] Article 15: In times of war, mobilization, or a state of emergency, the exercise of fundamental rights and freedoms may be partially or entirely suspended or measures derogating the guarantees embodied in the Constitution may be taken to the extent required by the exigencies of the situation, as long as obligations under international law are not violated.

Even under the circumstances indicated in the first paragraph, the individual's right to life, and the integrity of his/her material and spiritual existence shall be inviolable except where death occurs through acts in conformity with the law of war; no one shall be compelled to reveal his/her religion, conscience, thought or opinion, nor be accused on account of them; offenses and penalties shall not be made retroactive; nor shall anyone be held guilty until so proven by a court ruling.

[96] E.1990/25, K.1991/1, 10.01.1991; E.1991/6, K.1991/20, 03.07.1991; E.2003/28, K.2003/42, 22.05.2003.

In 2003, the Constitutional Court expanded the scope of its previous decisions. The court ruled that the government's power to issue emergency decree-laws is not only limited by articles 121 and 122 of the Constitution but also by other relevant provisions. The court interpreted the phrase 'matters necessitated by the state of emergency' in Article 121 broadly, taking into consideration all constitutional rules related to emergencies. In these three cases, the Court declared certain provisions of emergency decree-laws unconstitutional for exceeding the constitutional limits.[97]This precedent of the Court made a significant contribution to protect fundamental rights and freedoms in emergency regimes.

However, not all courts are eager to interfere with the executive's broad discretionary powers during emergencies. For example, the Supreme Court is not significantly effective in Argentina, even though the country has been under a permanent economic state of emergency for almost a century. Throughout decades, the Argentine Supreme Court has rubber-stamped the emergency measures, admitting in some cases clear violations of the constitutional rights, even if the requirements for the declaration of the emergency were not met. The court has never analyzed the real causes of the economic emergency or the reasonableness of the measures in light of the causes, so the court has acted as if this matter would have been excluded from judicial review.[98] Accordingly, following the constitutional reform of 1994, in the case of *Rodríguez,* the court declined to review the constitutionality of decrees of necessity and urgency. It reasoned that the Constitution (Section 99(3)) establishes a specific legislative oversight mechanism for such decrees, for which reason the intervention of the judicial power is not justified.[99] Unlike the approach adopted by the Colombian Constitutional Court, the Argentine Supreme Court deems that the provisional nature of a state of emergency cannot be fixed beforehand in a precise number of years or months. The temporal scope of the emergency depends on the continued existence of the circumstances that gave rise to it.[100] However, this approach may be criticized for failing to provide adequate safeguards to ensure that the executive remains within constitutional limits during periods of emergency.

Also, the Turkish Constitutional Court recently changed its case-law explained above. In 2016, the court unanimously rejected applications claiming the unconstitutionality of emergency decree-laws issued by the government follow-

---

[97] *Merih Öden* and *Selin Esen* (2016). Fundamental Rights and Freedoms in Turkey and the Turkish Constitutional Court. The Convergence of the Fundamental Rights Protections in Europe. Springer.

[98] *Juan Santiago Ylarri* (2021). "Permanent Economic Emergency in Argentina And Its Constitutional Implications". Mexican Law Review XIII(2): 103.

[99] CSJN, 17/12/1997, 'Rodríguez, Jorge' en: 'Nieva, Alejandro y otros c/ Poder Ejecutivo Nacional', Fallos (1997–320–2851).

[100] *Nadur*, Fallos (1959–243–449); *Guida*, Fallos (2000–323–1566). *Ylarri* (2021) (n. 98): 113.

ing the proclamation of the state of emergency due to a coup attempt.[101] In these judgments, maintaining its previous stance, the Court noted that the state of emergency in democratic countries is not an arbitrary regime. The primary objective of emergency regimes must be to guard and defend the constitutional order. Judicial control of all administrative acts and actions is an integral part of the principle of the rule of law. However, the Constitutional Court applied a literalist interpretation method while assessing Article 148.1 of the Constitution, which prohibits constitutional review of the emergency decree-laws. The court also examined the original intent of the framers of the Constitution, concluding that they intended to establish only parliamentary oversight over emergency decree-laws.

The Constitutional Court's rationale in these judgments appears to be self-contradictory. On the one hand, the Court still recognizes its discretionary power to designate the nature of a legal text and to determine whether it falls within the scope of the constitutional review. On the other hand, it asserts that such a designation regarding the nature of a rule should not lead to a constitutional review of an emergency decree-law. Otherwise, Article 148.1 of the Constitution, which explicitly prohibits the constitutional review of emergency decree-laws, would lose its significance. According to the Court, reviewing the constitutionality of emergency decree-laws would also infringe upon Article 11 of the Constitution, which emphasizes the supremacy and binding effect of the Constitution, and Article 6, which prohibits individuals and state organs from exercising state authority that does not emanate from the Constitution. However, the Constitutional Court disregards the fact that the counterview is equally valid. In other words, the court`s rationale gives the executive absolute discretionary power to issue any measure via emergency decree-laws, such as suspending all constitutional rights and freedoms without regard to constitutional limitations or even abolition of all democratic institutions, including the court itself .[102] It seems that the court disregards one of the fundamental functions of the constitutional courts, which is to maintain the supremacy and binding effect of the Constitution by controlling the constitutionality of laws or other norms having the force of law. Still, a constitutional court must interpret the constitution as a whole and embrace a rights-based approach. This requires the Court to read constitutional limitations regarding rights and freedoms as narrowly as possible. Consequently, the court's judgments appear detrimental for the rule of law, where the primary objective is to limit the government and safeguard rights and freedoms.

[101] E.2016/166, K.2016/159, 12.10. 2016; E.2016/167, K.2016/160, 12.10. 2016; E.2016/171, K.2016/164, 02.11. 2016; E.2016/172 K.2016/165, 02.11. 2016.

[102] *Selin Esen* (2016). 'Judicial Control of the Decree-Laws in Emergency Regimes: A self-Destruction Attempt of the Turkish Constitutional Court?'. https://iacl-aidc-blog.org/2016/12/19/judicial-control-of-the-decree-laws-in-emergency-regimes-a-self-destruction-attempt-by-the-turkish-constitutional-court/.

F. Conclusion

The distinction between the Global South and the Global North is far from monolithic. Countries in both blocs encompass a wide array of economic, political, and geopolitical diversities. The use of catch-all labels risks reinforcing inaccurate and *outdated dichotomies* and stereotypes, at the expense of recognizing the world in all of its varieties. These diversities can, blur the North-South dichotomy or reveal distinctions within each bloc.

In many fields, including the rule of law, there is notable cross-fertilization between the North and the South. For instance, the concept of the rights of nature, which originated in the Global South, appropriates ideas from the Global North, namely the European notion of human rights, and integrates them with non-western, indigenous cosmovisions of nature. Countries in the Global North benefit from these alternative conceptions of nature and rights through intercultural exchanges to address environmental issues.[103] This emergence of a distinct legal paradigm, based on the principle of 'relationality' from indigenous jurisprudence and political movements in the Global South,[104] fosters dialogue on the rule of law from a communitarian and decolonial perspective. It promotes the integration of non-Western perspectives from the Global South into the Western tradition of the rule of law.

Moreover, there exists an interrelationship within the Global South itself. For example, the striking resemblance between Section 73 of the 2013 Constitution of Zimbabwe and Article 24 of the 1996 Constitution of South Africa regarding environmental rights illustrates how legal ideas can transcend in the region. Likewise, Ecuador's Constitutional Court deemed in 2009 that Ecuador's new constitution represents "a departure from the classic anthropocentric conception, by which the human is the center and aim of all things, and brings us closer to an ecocentric vision that acknowledges our interdependence with nature." This perspective reflects the Asiatic lion and wild buffalo decisions of India's Supreme Court.[105]

High-profile, activist courts have expanded in recent years in both the North and the South. Indeed, countries such as India, Colombia, and South Africa have emerged as significant contributors to the discourse on liberal democratic principles, such as socioeconomic rights, access to justice, and have taken pioneering steps to address environmental issues. Many countries in the South have become key participants in the evolving concept of liberal democratic constitutional-

---

[103] *Boaventura de Sousa* Santos (2017). A New Version of Europe: Learning from the South", European Cosmopolitanism. Colonial Histories and Postcolonial Societies *(*eds. Gurminder K. Bhambra and John Narayan*)*. Routledge: 180.

[104] *Maria Elena Attard Bellido* (2019). Entre la diosa Themis y Mama Ocllo: la propuesta de argumentación jurídica plural desde la filosofía intercultural andina de la Chakana. Diálogos de Saberes 50: 79.

[105] *Boyd* (2017) (n. 36): 242.

ism.[106] Although the Global South produces intriguing original remedies in the field of the rule of law, significant challenges persist in enforcing the rule of law within its diverse sociopolitical contexts, often marked by postcolonial legacies and uneven development.[107] Nonetheless, the rich tapestry of legal innovation, particularly regarding social and environmental rights, signals an evolving understanding of constitutionalism that transcends traditional dichotomies. Consequently, the legal experiences from the Global South present not just challenges but also opportunities for enriching the global dialogue on the rule of law.

[106] *Rosalind Dixon* and *David Landau* (2021). Abusive Constitutional Borrowing. Oxford University Press: 11.

[107] *López Zamora* (n. 39): 481; Deva (n. 46): 40; *Erin Daly* and *James R. May* (eds.) (2018). Implementing Environmental Constitutionalism: Current Global Challenges. Cambridge University Press: 7; *May* (n. 50): 1012.

Socio-Economic Rights – Between the Global South and Global North

David Bilchitz

A. Introduction

Socio-economic rights are universal in nature. They are rooted in the recognition of the dignity of individuals and that individuals require certain resources to be treated in accordance with their dignity. It is thus not surprising that these rights are recognised in the Universal Declaration of Human Rights ('UNDHR'), the first instrument to proclaim fundamental rights as a foundation for the new post-Second World War global order. That Declaration recognises the right to social security and the 'realisation…of the economic, social and cultural rights indispensable for his dignity and the free development of his personality.'[1] It also recognises further socio-economic rights such as a right to work (article 23), to rest and leisure (article 24), to a standard of living adequate for health and well-being (article 25) and to education (article 26). These are presumably all entitlements that every individual needs to live a life of dignity and to flourish by their own rights. Socio-economic rights have also been enshrined in the binding International Covenant on Economic, Social and Cultural Rights ('ICESCR').[2]

At the same time, even within this universal recognition of socio-economic rights, there are immediately qualifiers which place a degree of relativity into the obligations that flow from these rights. For instance, article 22 states the following:

> 'Everyone, as a member of society, has the right to social security and is entitled to realization, through national effort and international co-operation *and in accordance with the organization and resources of each State,* of the economic, social and cultural rights indispensable for his dignity and the free development of his personality.' (Emphasis added).[3]

Individuals are only entitled to the realisation of economic, social and cultural rights 'in accordance with the organisation and resources of each state'. Since the

---

[1] See the Universal Declaration of Human Rights, 10 December 1948 UN (available at: https://www.un.org/en/about-us/universal-declaration-of-human-rights accessed at 07.04.2025).

[2] International Covenant on Economic, Social and Cultural Rights, 16 December 1966 (available at: https://www.ohchr.org/en/instruments-mechanisms/instruments/international-covenant-economic-social-and-cultural-rights accessed at 07.04.2025).

[3] UNDHR (note 1 above).

organisation and resources of each state vary significantly across the world, there is thus a recognition even in this earlier encapsulation of significant variation that will take place in the realisation of these rights. Such relativity is also captured in the main general obligation included in article 2(1) of the ICESCR:

'Each State Party to the present Covenant undertakes to take steps, individually and through international assistance and co-operation, especially economic and technical, to the maximum of *its available resources*, with a view to achieving progressively the full realization of the rights recognized in the present Covenant by all appropriate means, including particularly the adoption of legislative measures.' (Emphasis added).[4]

The obligation here is upon each state party to take steps to the maximum of its available resources to achieve progressively the full realisation of these rights. The provision assumes there will be different levels of resources available to different states and, presumably, progressive realisation will mean different levels of realisation given these different levels of resources.

Thus, built into the very recognition of socio-economic rights is both a firm statement of their universality but also a relativisation of the obligations they impose to the capacity and resources of individual states. Such qualifications are generally not included in relation to civil and political rights – even where they implicate resources.

We know that there is a significant resource disparity between countries across the globe. Countries are often classified in relation to this disparity. Originally, there was a clear division drawn between 'first' and 'third' world and so-called 'developed' and 'developing' countries which partially relate to levels of socio-economic rights realisation. More recently, the terminology has shifted to a focus on the divide between the Global North and between the Global South. This is not a geographical division given some global north countries are in fact in the south of the globe – such as Australia – and global south countries may be in the north of the globe – such as India and China. The divide has a historical dimension: Southern countries generally have a shared experience of colonialism whereas Northern countries were the colonizers. That, in turn, has had a number of important continuing effects in the present: 'political effects' relate to the governance of those societies with Southern countries; 'economic effects' relate to the distribution of wealth in those societies; and 'epistemic effects' which relate to what constitutes valuable knowledge and who produces it.[5]

This article will elaborate on this distinction in the sections below. Whilst recognising that there are significant differences between countries in the Global South and Global North, the article accepts that the distinction roughly captures an important divide. The focus of this article is on socio-economic rights and, in particular, the judicial enforcement thereof. The article will also focus on a par-

[4] Article 2(1) of the ICESCR (note 2 above).

[5] *Dann* The Global South and Comparative Constitutional Law (Oxford University Press, 2020) 6 at 16–17.

ticular sub-set of these rights, namely, what I term 'subsistence rights' such as the right to food, housing, water and health-care.[6] The question, at the heart of this article, is, whether the broad categories of the Global North and Global South are illuminating when examining the adjudication of socio-economic rights. In other words, are judges faced with broadly the same task when adjudicating these rights in the Global North and Global South, or, given the differences in resources and governance between these two contexts, does adjudication involve quite different enterprises? In answering this question, it is of course necessary to consider a range of sub-questions: If the task of judges is different in these two contexts, how does it affect our understanding of the appropriate judicial role – in light of the separation of powers – in these contexts? Moreover, if the task is different, how does it affect the approach that has been adopted towards giving content to these rights? Similarly, if the task is different, what impact does this have on the remedies that flow from these rights? Lastly, how does this analysis affect the ability to compare the jurisprudence between these contexts?

In addressing these questions, this article will proceed as follows. In the first part, it will focus on the Global North. In doing so, it will seek to determine key distinguishing features of Global North societies. It will then divide the analysis into three parts: First, it will seek to understand whether and why socio-economic rights are important in Global North countries and what justification exists for judges to enforce these rights there; that will affect our understanding of the task of judges in these societies. It will then consider what effect that justification has on the approach judges adopt towards determining the content of rights as well as the remedies they grant. The article will focus on a qualitative analysis of the *Hartz IV* judgment in Germany to illustrate some of these key themes.[7]

The second part of the article will shift to the context of the Global South and elaborate upon key elements of these societies that distinguish them from the North – in this context, differences in resources and government capacity play a key role. In a parallel manner to the first part, it will then turn to understand the justification that exists there for judges to enforce these right and the task they are assigned. It will utilise this understanding to examine approaches that have been adopted to determining the content of these rights as well as remedies. It will identify a difference in approach in two different Global South societies, and to illustrate these differences it will contrast the *T-025 of 2004* decision of the Co-

[6] Socio-economic rights are often clustered together but include a range of rights with different bases including rights to work, to join a trade union, to education and much else in addition: See *Jung, Hirschl and Rosevear* 'Economic and Social Rights in National Constitutions' (2014) 62 American Journal of Comparative Law 1043 at 1054–1055, who categorise the rights in distinct categories. I wish to focus on a sub-category of rights I term 'subsistence rights' which relate to the resources necessary for individuals to function and achieve their goals – these include rights to housing, food, water and health-care (a different categorisation to the above authors).

[7] 125 BVerfGE 175, 1 BVL 1/09 of 9 February 2010 ('*Hartz IV*').

lombian Constitutional Court relating to internally displaced persons;[8] with the *Grootboom* decision of the South African Constitutional Court relating to the provision of housing to those in desperate need.[9]

Finally, this article will conclude with some reflections on the usefulness of the categories of the Global North and Global South in the context of the adjudication of socio-economic rights. In particular, in light of the analysis and differences in task and context, I will reflect on the perils of comparing the jurisprudence on socio-economic rights between the Global North and Global South. I will seek to illustrate why, for instance, a Northern conception of the separation of powers is particularly harmful and disruptive in hampering and undermining the enforcement of socio-economic rights in the Global South. Thus, I shall contend that comparative constitutional law scholarship, in this area, has a rather complex task: It must unflinchingly defend the universality of socio-economic rights whilst recognising that the different contexts of the Global South and Global North justifiably affect the legal approaches to be adopted towards their realisation.

B. Socio-Economic Rights in the Global North

I. Key Characteristics of Global North Countries

As has been mentioned, historically, many of the Global North countries were colonizers. Others were connected in economic relationships with those that were colonizers. That allowed them to exploit the wealth of the colonized countries to enhance the wealth of their residents as well as internal living standards. Thus, the GDP per capita in Global North countries was $ 58,825 in 2025 – whereas in the Global South, it was $ 19,098. That means there are greater levels of resources that can be spent on each individual in those societies in improving their access to socio-economic rights. There are also smaller populations in the Global North (1,642 million in Global North versus 6,171 million in the Global South), allowing for a greater amount of resources to be distributed amongst a smaller population base. The Global North also has, as a result, a much higher average life expectancy (77,9 in Global North versus 67,9 in Global South) but also aging populations (the average median age is 39,3 in the Global North versus 24,7 in the Global South). This economic disparity also affects political governance. The Global North countries are often stable democracies with limited corruption, and protection for civil and political rights. Their states are also capable and broadly deliver services and resources for those who live within their borders and do not divert large amounts of resources to corruption. In terms of a governance

[8] Colombian Constitutional Court, Decision *No. T-025 of 2004*.

[9] *Government of the Republic of South Africa v Grootboom* [2000] ZACC 19 ('*Grootboom*').

index that aggregates the rule of law, press freedom, political rights and corruption perceptions, 51 % of countries in the Global North have an A governance rating and 26 % a B governance rating whereas only 3 % in the Global South have an A governance rating and 18 % a B rating.[10] Of course there are differences between countries within these categories but the clear picture that emerges is of a segment of the world where, on the whole living standards are decent and there is stable, relatively efficient governance.

II. The Justification for Judicial Enforcement of Socio-Economic Rights

Given this data, the question may arise then as to what the point of socio-economic rights is in these countries. Historically, fundamental rights originated in the Constitutions of the Global North in struggles against political repression and authoritarianism. For this reason, the focus of the early declarations of fundamental rights was on civil and political rights.[11] Many Global North countries thus did not include socio-economic rights within their Constitutions. Indeed, of the 16 countries, where socio-economic rights are absent, most of these are Global North countries.[12] Data indicates a low level of prevalence of socio-economic rights and, particularly, subsistence rights in the Constitutions of Western Europe and North America.[13] As will be evident below in relation to Germany, socio-economic rights have, at times, been interpreted by Constitutional Courts into existing Constitutions through other rights like dignity.[14]

Some authors have suggested that these countries 'have high levels of economic development and many also have well-established social welfare institutions that may make economic and social rights seem redundant'.[15] Yet, despite good aggregate data, it is clear that there have been rising distributional inequalities within Global North countries as well. For instance, in the United States, the richest 10 % earn around 45 % of the income; in Germany, this figure is around

[10] For all the statistics in this paragraph, see 'Global North' (August 2025) World Economics (available at: https://www.worldeconomics.com/Regions/Global-North/ accessed at 25.08.2025).

[11] The first declaration of rights was the French Declaration of the Rights of Man and of the Citizen in August 1789 (available at: https://avalon.law.yale.edu/18th_century/rightsof.asp accessed at 07.04.2025). This was followed shortly thereafter by the amendments to the United States Constitution which took effect in December 1791.

[12] The data here is taken from *Jung, Hirschl and Rosevear* (note 6 above). These countries are: Australia, Brunei, Canada, France, Israel, Kiribati, Lebanon, Liechtenstein, Malaysia, Micronesia, New Zealand, Singapore, Tonga, Trinidad and Tobago, the United States, and Vanuatu.

[13] Ibid. at 1078–1079.

[14] See *Leitjen* Core Socio-Economic Rights and the European Court of Human Rights (Cambridge University Press, 2018) on the European Court of Human Rights' interpretation of civil and political rights to include some protection for socio-economic rights.

[15] *Jung, Hirschl and Rosevear* (note 6 above) at 1079.

35 % and in the UK around 33 %.[16] These disparities mean that the average data relating to high levels of GDP in these countries does not adequately capture how the resources are distributed within these societies. Whilst some are very well off, others can be very badly off. In these Global North societies, in general, there are large middle classes and so the majority of individuals are in a reasonably well-off position. That, in turn, leads to a situation where the majority of voting citizens are in conditions were broadly they are able to provide for their own socio-economic subsistence needs such as food, and housing and so need not claim these entitlements from the state. For this reason, those who are not able to provide for these needs are a relatively small minority whose interests differ from those of the majority – there is thus a lack of political focus on those interests. Some socio-economic interests which affect the majority may well be quite central to democratic debates – such as around health and education, though, once again, they often relate to improving conditions for those reasonably well-off rather than addressing those suffering from the most severe forms of deprivation (such as poorly performing schools for those who are the most vulnerable). Socio-economic rights require that every individual is entitled to the resources necessary for living lives of dignity and which enable them to flourish. They also require particular attention to the urgent interests of those who are most vulnerable. Where majoritarian institutions are not likely adequately to address and protect these rights – or pay attention to the interests of those whose needs are most urgent – there is a need for an alternative institution to ensure that these entitlements are realised. Such institutions may take various forms but, in the absence of any other institution, it is the judiciary which is tasked with defending rights and correcting for failures of democracy to take account of the interests of a vulnerable minority who lacks access to basic resources. In any event, this justification would provide good normative reasons for socio-economic rights to be protected in Global North constitutions – which often fail to do so – and for the judiciary to interpret existing constitutions to include protection for such rights.[17]

It is evident that this justification for judicial enforcement of socio-economic rights is no different to the justification for judicial involvement in enforcing civil and political rights. It involves one of the classic answers to the famous counter-majoritarian dilemma: why should unelected judges have the power to impose their decisions on elected branches? A common response is that democratic processes have various flaws and that majoritarian democracy essentially can lead to the under-protection of the rights of minorities.[18] Judicial enforcement of rights

---

[16] See *Qureshi* 'Rising Inequality: A Major Issue of Our Time' (16 May 2023) Brookings at figure 1 (available at: https://www.brookings.edu/articles/rising-inequality-a-major-issue-of-our-time/ accessed at 07.04.2025).

[17] *Bilchitz* 'Are Socio-Economic Rights a Form of Political Rights' (2015) 31 South African Journal on Human Rights 86.

[18] Famously, these arguments were foreshadowed by the majority in footnote 4 of *United States v Carolene Products* 304 US 144 (1938); *Ely* Democracy and Distrust (Harvard University Press, 1981) 135 ff.

helps to correct for these systemic flaws and ensure that the interests of those who would not be adequately protected are properly addressed. Minorities need not just be those with particular identities that have been discriminated against – such as individuals on grounds of race, sex or sexual orientation – but can also involve those marginalised due to their socio-economic status. Socio-economic rights thus have an important role to play in developed Global North countries in ensuring the interests of vulnerable socio-economic minorities are protected. This rationale also indicates that they do not raise particular worries relating to judicial review any different to those that arise in relation to civil and political rights.

An illustration of this point, for instance, can be given in relation to my own experience of working on homelessness in the UK during my time as a graduate student in Cambridge. I was rather surprised and shocked to discover many people sleeping on the streets in the very cold winters (referred to in the UK as sleeping rough). I was part of an organisation that engaged with authorities about the problem. What became clear was that a new shelter was required to house the people sleeping rough but the elected local council representatives would not co-operate to make this happen. The reason for this was that many middle-class people were opposed to having a homeless shelter near their homes and the greatest number of electorally significant votes were amongst the middle class. As a result, given the small number of homeless people on the streets and their lack of political organisation, there was no political incentive for elected representatives to challenge the majority of their base – and risk losing their seats – and protect the rights of these vulnerable people. Such a situation, demonstrates why electoral politics alone cannot protect the socio-economic rights of the most vulnerable even in highly developed countries where resources are plentiful and governments are generally capable.

An interesting judicial decision in this regard is the *Hartz IV* judgment in Germany.[19] The decision related to the unemployment benefit in Germany which consisted of a standard benefit to secure one's livelihood as well as subsidies for accommodation and heating. A legislative amendment reduced the benefit by 10% and sought to determine the amount to be granted by tying it to changes in the amount paid out in pensions. The benefit of children was also calculated as a percentage of an adult's benefit. The constitutionality of the reduction of the benefits – and the methods of calculation thereof – was challenged in the Constitutional Court of Germany and the Court ultimately found these changes to be unconstitutional. The case is an example of where a democratically elected legislature reduced the benefits of a minority of economic vulnerable individuals in society. The rationale discussed above for judicial intervention is thus clear but, there is a need to consider in more detail, in what manner the judiciary should go about giving effect to the enforcement of these rights. I consider two issues: the

[19] *Hartz IV* judgment (note 7 above).

question of the content to be attributed to these rights, as well as the remedies that should be given when they are infringed. A central issue that arises in relation to both issues has been the separation of powers and what role the judiciary should play in giving effect to these rights. I consider the *Hartz IV* decision as an illustration of the issues involved and an approach adopted by a leading Constitutional Court in the Global North.

III. The Judicial Role in Developing the Content of Socio-Economic Rights

It has been mentioned that many Global North countries do not in fact include socio-economic rights in their Constitutions and, where they do, do not provide for the judicial enforcement thereof. Nevertheless, there have been a number of examples of increasing judicial enforcement in the Global North particularly within Europe and sometimes, the use of civil and political rights to find at least a minimum level of protection for socio-economic rights.[20] The question I am interested in here is, given the broad political and economic dimensions of the Global North, what broad approach is justifiable when it comes to the judiciary giving content to socio-economic rights? As before, there is naturally a disclaimer that what is said here may vary with the particular circumstances of particular countries.

Broadly, Global North countries have relatively established constitutional courts whose orders are respected. Given the commitment to the rule of law, even if there is disagreement with the orders of a court, they tend to be obeyed. It is thus not a serious concern of the courts to establish their institutional security[21] or, in their reasoning to be concerned about whether or not their orders will be followed. These considerations mean that courts in the Global North can develop the content of socio-economic rights without a concern about their orders being disobeyed.

The general availability of significant resources means that resource considerations need play less of a role when giving content to these rights. That also has an important implication for how the content thereof is determined – particularly, in relation to subsistence rights. In reasonably well-off societies, there is no significant need for prioritisation amongst those whose subsistence rights are not realised. As we saw, the ICESCR speaks about the progressive realisation of socio-economic rights, which assumes resource constraints that prevent the full realisation of these rights. Since such constraints are limited in Global North countries – except perhaps in relation to health care which is a special case – there is no strong need to have different tiers for the realisation of these rights, some of which have priority over others. Thus, courts in the Global North can, in some

[20] See *Leitjen* (note 14 above).

[21] This contrasts with the position in the Global South – see Roux 'Principle and Pragmatism on the Constitutional Court of South Africa' (2009) 7 International Journal of Constitutional Law 107 at 109.

senses, be more ambitious in ensuring the full realisation of these rights and do not have to worry about prioritisation between the vulnerable.

These considerations would support a more expansive approach to the adjudication of socio-economic rights in the Global North. At the same time, as has been mentioned, the state in these countries is understood to have greater expertise in determining social and economic policy. Judges, who may be experts in fundamental rights, may lack expertise in that regard and the modalities of giving effect to the realisation of these rights. Moreover, there may be an established and vibrant democratic political culture for debating policy in this regard – which may mean that the political community is less willing for judges to make decisions that can be made through political processes. These considerations do not oust the case for judicial involvement – however, they provide some grounds for a more restrained role.[22] One possibility is for judges to provide general direction on the standards to be given effect to in realising these rights but not being overly prescriptive in determining the exact quantitative amount necessary to give effect to these standards. Thus, in this way, separation of powers concerns are taken account of in a consideration of what content should be granted to these rights.

The *Hartz IV* decision can help illuminate many of these dynamics at play. The German Constitutional Court is well established and respected within Germany and has no fear about its orders being disobeyed. It, significantly in this decision, recognises explicitly that there is a fundamental guarantee to a subsistence minimum in Germany – which it derives from the right to dignity read together with the principle of the social state.[23] The latter principle requires the legislature to establish such a minimum though the legislature is granted a margin of appreciation in determining the quantity of resources that gives effect to that.[24] The legislature is required to guarantee the right though it has some latitude in giving concrete effect to it. The Court explicates that the guarantee involves protection for the means that are vital to an existence in line with human dignity. That involves two components: A guarantee that encompasses the physical existence of individuals – goods such as food, clothing, housing etc. – as well as the 'possibility to maintain inter-human relationships and a minimum of participation in social, cultural and political life, given that humans as persons of necessity exist in social relationships'.[25]

The Court, thus, clearly is confident enough to set the constitutional standard or goal which legislative action must achieve. At the same time, it grants a significant margin of appreciation to the legislature to give concrete effect to this

[22] *Dixon* Responsive Judicial Review: Democracy and Dysfunction in the Modern Age (Oxford University Press, 2023) 6.

[23] *Egidy* 'The Fundamental Right to the Guarantee of a Subsistence Minimum in the *Hartz IV* Decision of the German Federal Constitutional Court' (2011) 12 German Law Journal 1961 at 1969.

[24] *Hartz IV* judgment (note 7 above) at para C(I)(1).

[25] Ibid. at para C(I)(i)(b).

right. In particular, the finding in this case is that the statistical and procedural methods to assess what constitutes the subsistence minimum were unjustifiable on several grounds. For instance, the reductions in benefits were calculated on the basis of goods that people who are vulnerable may not utilise – such as camping furniture, works of art and sports-boats. Moreover, the calculation of benefits for children on the basis of a blanket percentage of adult needs was not related to the actual needs of children. Linking the subsistence minimum to changes in pensions was also not justifiable given different factors were relevant to pensions and the subsistence minimum. The Court, found that it was not its role to determine a particular quantifiable amount to which each person was entitled:[26] Rather, it set the general standard and the parameters for the exercise of legislative power as well as indicating a duty on the legislature to justify its methodology, which includes a duty to be consistent and to be transparent.[27]

In attempting to capture what lies within the existence minimum, the Court includes not just physical existence but also higher-level goods that enable individuals to participate in society. At the same time, the court recognises a degree of priority between these two elements of the minimum: the discretion of the legislature is narrower in relation to physical existence and wider in relation to the social component.[28] Arguably, this recognises the greater degree of urgency that physical existence elements have: In a country like Germany, both are realisable, however, and so are included in the social minimum.

IV. The Judicial Role in Granting Remedies in Respect of Socio-Economic Rights

Remedies in the Global North can, on the one hand, be strong:[29] The institutional position of the court is secure, resources are available and the capacity to implement can be assumed. At the same time, in systems with stronger democratic pedigrees and a more functional democratic sphere, the role of the judiciary is understood to be more limited and a degree of deference is required to the elected arms of government. Remedies thus need to balance the strong position of such courts with not overstepping the limits and understanding of the judicial role in that society.

The *Hartz IV* decision illustrates this in practice. The Court is confident to outline what is required by the right to an existence minimum. It is also willing to consider whether the legislature has adopted a consistent and justifiable method for determining that minimum. At the same time, it does not seek quantitatively to determine the amount of that minimum or determine the exact method for

---

[26] Ibid. at para D(I)(i).

[27] *Egidy* (note 23 above) at 1978–1981.

[28] *Hartz IV* judgment (note 7 above) at para C(I)(d).

[29] For the division between strong and weak content and remedies, see *Tushnet* Weak Courts, Strong Rights: Judicial Review and Social Welfare Rights in Comparative Constitutional Law (Princeton University Press, 2008) 249–250.

such a determination. It thus declares the reduction in benefits and legislative changes to be unconstitutional due to a failure to adopt a justifiable method to assess that reduction. This is a relatively strong remedy which invalidates a legislative scheme. At the same time, the court does not replace the scheme with one of its own devising. It defers to the legislature to adopt a justifiable method for quantifying the amount of the benefit. It also does not apply the declaration retrospectively, but only prospectively: its reasoning demonstrates a sensitivity to a possible unanticipated fiscal impact. It also relates to the fact that the case does not establish a manifest failure to realise the right to a subsistence minimum but rather a failure in the method of calculation. This type of remedy can be seen to be a type of weaker and more dialogic one: The court feeds back to the legislature that its method of calculation was not justifiable and requires a modification in this regard.

The court, however, adopts a stronger stance in relation to special needs that are current and irrefutable. The costs of these special needs have to be instituted immediately prior to legislative consideration – the court reasons that, given the failure to provide for these needs can lead to a serious violation of dignity, they have to be provided for immediately. There is, once again, here a recognition of urgency of the impact on dignity and the potential for harm to those who are vulnerable. Where that potential is manifest and a gap can seriously harm such individuals, less deference is accorded to the legislature. Presumably, also, given the limited number of people to whom this applies, in these cases, the budgetary impact would be less.

We thus see, in this decision, the court being able to exercise strong remedial powers but also expressly stepping back from doing so, where it is concerned about the effects on the fiscus and intruding too deeply on the discretion of democratic branches. Given the other branches are understood to act in good faith and be capable, there is no fear of the need to replace their decision-making with that of the court. The court retains its role as a standard-setter in relation to rights with the legislature having to give effect to these standards in concrete legislation.

C. The Global South and Socio-Economic Rights

I. Key Characteristics

I have already outlined the statistics of Global North countries vis-à-vis the Global South countries. I will here summarise some of the key features that characterise Global South countries on the whole. The first historical dimension is the fact that they were colonised and so had many of their resources exploited, their people subjugated and their knowledge systems and systems of governance interfered with. These dimensions have all had lasting effects on the societies and many are still struggling to overcome the legacy of colonialism. The economic effects are seen in the fact that many of the Global South countries have much weaker economies with less developed industrial capacity and high levels of unemployment. Many have large populations with fewer resources being available per individual. Individuals, on the whole, have less access to socio-economic goods and the infrastructure of systems such as healthcare and education are not well-developed. For these reasons, one sees a lower life expectancy in these countries. The level of need is thus very great across most Global South countries and yet the resources that are available per capita are much more limited than in Global North countries.

These economic problems are accompanied by political ones. Many of these countries had their traditional modes of governance interfered with and after the departure of the colonial power, have struggled to attain stable and democratic government. Many of these countries are authoritarian and not real democracies. Those countries which are truly democratic remain in a state where the architecture of democracy is being built and emerging: institutions in those societies thus need to build their legitimacy and pedigree. Unfortunately, Global South countries have also experienced an epidemic of corruption which has led to a diversion of resources from addressing the needs of individuals to the pockets of corrupt politicians and government officials. Many of the post-colonial states have also not established expert non-political civil services – in many countries, government bureaucracies have been corrupted with appointments that are not meritocratic and based on loyalty to the ruling elite. This has led to a crisis in the capacity of many of the Global South states to deliver the services that their residents require. Thus, even if there were adequate resources, there is a significant lack of ability to deliver on the rights, expectations and needs of residents.

II. The Justification for the Judicial Enforcement of Socio-Economic Rights

As we saw, the justification for judicial enforcement of socio-economic rights in Global North countries is very much related to the failures of majoritarian democracy to protect the rights of vulnerable minorities. Where the majority are reasonably well-off, the socio-economic rights of the vulnerable may require a non-majoritarian institution to correct for these failures in democracy. It is no doubt true that this justification will also be partially applicable in the Global South as well – there are no doubt vulnerable groups who are not adequately catered to by majoritarian institutions and whose rights may be significantly imperilled without a non-majoritarian corrective. Nevertheless, in the Global South, this is not the only justification for judicial involvement in enforcing socio-economic rights and the justification extends beyond this traditional response to the counter-majoritarian dilemma.

Indeed, one major assumption underlying arguments against judicial review that have been made by Jeremy Waldron is that democratic institutions are 'in reasonably good working order'.[30] The problem in many Global South societies is that this assumption is unwarranted and there are deep flaws in the representative democratic structures that exist. It may be that the society is highly stratified leading to voting patterns along lines of ethnicity (such as in Kenya). It may be that there is a one-party dominant state such as where a liberation party is voted in continuously for many years (such as happened in South Africa until recently). It may be that the incumbent skews the democratic system to their advantage (such as an India) or that there is an inability to arrive at stable governance where no party has a majority (such as in local government in South Africa). There also may be a significant disconnect between the elected representatives – who are reasonably well-off – and their constituents who are not. In the Global South, thus, there may be a need to correct for failures in the democratic system that affect the majority and not just the minority. There is also a historic difficulty of organising those who are not well-off such that their interests are adequately taken into account in the political sphere. Populist parties may fill this void and adopt what sound like simple solutions that will have dire effects on the poor. Judicial involvement may thus be required to correct for these additional failures in democratic institutions that are needed to ensure the interests of the majority are protected.

There has also been a significant problem of corruption both in the legislature and executive. Corruption means that these institutions do not perform their tasks that they are assigned in the constitutional scheme and fail to act for the public good. As such, there is a diversion of resources from the needy to the corrupt. The judiciary has a role to play here not only in criminally convicting those who are proved to be corrupt but also to ensure that decision-making is justifiable in the interests of the governed. These include further tasks such as ensuring that procurement processes are fair and that value for money for the governed is realised.

In relation to the executive, there often is a lack of capacity to develop and give effect to government policy with no historical administrative state, the departure of skills (sometimes to the Global North or the private sector) and the lack of adequate skills in society. The lack of capacity entails that there is no assumption that the executive can perform its planning role or give effect to the plans it makes. To ensure socio-economic rights are realised, there will, at times, be a need for another state organ (such as the judiciary) to exercise a supervisory role to ensure policies are developed and given effect to.[31] There may also be a legacy of

[30] *Waldron* 'The Core of the Case Against Judicial Review' (2006) 115 Yale Law Journal 1346 at 1360.

[31] See *Young* 'The Avoidance of Substance in Constitutional Rights' (2013) 5 Constitutional Court Review 233 at 238–239; *Taylor* 'Forcing the Court's Remedial Hand: Non-Compliance as a Catalyst for Remedial Innovation' (2019) 9 Constitutional Court Review 247 at 253; *Nthenya* 'The Place of Structural Interdicts In The Enforcement of Social Economic Rights In Kenya' (15 February 2022) SSRN (available at: https://ssrn.com/abstract=4131623 accessed at 07.04.2025).

institutional cultures averse to performance: In such an instance, there may be a need to compel performance.[32]

The weakness of the state and the lack of ability on the part of the other branches to perform their roles creates a vacuum in the state that needs to be filled. It may well be that, recognising these problems, other institutions should be developed to address these weaknesses. In some countries, like South Africa, there has been some experimentation with fourth-branch institutions such as a Public Protector and Human Rights Commission. At the same time, many of the weaknesses facing the legislature and executive can bedevil these alternative institutions too. It seems inescapable thus that the judiciary will be called on to address some of the weaknesses in the other branches. Its role in the Global South is thus not only about protecting minorities but rather about enabling and compelling the performance of the basic tasks of the state.

The traditional separation of powers doctrine does not function well in this context. It is premised upon each branch of government performing their role well and that maximum efficiency will be obtained through dividing the state in this way.[33] Given the failures of efficiency of the legislature and executive, the question is what role remains for this doctrine? It is quite clear that the judiciary cannot become the sole, governing body of the state. Not only does it lack the legitimacy to do so but it also lacks the institutional make-up and structures necessary for this task. Judges have a particular legal training and background and the judiciary, in most states, is not set up to determine policy but to hear and adjudicate individual cases. The role and powers of the judiciary cannot be equivalent to that in the Global North where other branches are more-or-less functional – but, they also cannot take over the governance of the state. The separation of powers in the Global South needs to grapple with how the strengths of judicial institutions can be marshalled to catalyse, and compel the other branches to perform their functions and so deliver for the poor.[34] Their role is thus likely to be much more extensive than that in the Global North and involves playing a central role in the strengthening democratic institutions or other branches and holding them accountable. How that role is to be performed raises a number of conundrums and has led to differences in approach. It is also not helpful that the model of the separation of powers in the Global North is dominant and often transplanted without a consideration of context to the Global South. In the discussion below of the judicial approaches to determining the

---

[32] *Roach and Budlender* 'Mandatory and Supervisory Jurisdiction: When is it Appropriate, Just and Equitable?' (2005) 122 South African Law Journal 325 at 349; *Taylor* ibid. at 249–253.

[33] *Barber* 'Prelude to the Separation of Powers' (2001) 60 Cambridge Law Journal 59 ('the core of the doctrine is not liberty, as many writers have assumed, but efficiency').

[34] *Young* 'A Typology of Economic and Social Rights Adjudication: Exploring the Catalytic Function of Judicial Review' (2010) 8 International Journal of Constitutional Law 385 at 387.

content of socio-economic rights and remedies to be given, I will contrast the approach adopted in South Africa with that adopted in Colombia, which indicate some of the difficult choices for the judiciary in this context.

III. Approaches to Determining the Content of Socio-Economic Rights in the Global South

Two central elements are in great tension in Global South countries when deciding on the content to be given to socio-economic rights: the first is the level of need and the second is the limited resources available in these countries to address those needs. The conditions of need were aptly described by Chaskalson P in the *Soobramoney* case:

> 'Millions of people are living in deplorable conditions and in great poverty. There is a high level of unemployment, inadequate social security, and many do not have access to clean water or to adequate health services.'[35]

These high-levels of need and limited resources entail that the full realisation of these rights cannot be achieved immediately and that there are a range of pressing demands the state has to respond to which, at times, compete with one another. In the face of such large need and limited resources, what are judges to do with such rights to make them meaningful? I explore two approaches that have been adopted to address this problem.

1. Standard Setting and Prioritisation: Colombia

One approach which is similar to that in the Global North is to draw on the courts' expertise in the fundamental rights field in order to set standards for the realisation of these rights. To be meaningful however, such standards cannot be unrealistic and must grapple with the circumstances of limited resources. What is clear is that given these limited resources, the full realisation of these rights cannot take place immediately and, as a result, there will be need to be some principles for determining what is required pending full realisation. If these rights are recognised as individual rights, it cannot be that individuals can be allowed to perish in the interim; at the same time, the full realisation of these rights for all cannot take place immediately.

At the global level, this dilemma was addressed by the UN Committee on Economic, Social and Cultural Rights, when considering what is meant by the term 'progressive realisation' in the ICESCR. The Committee found that that states have a 'minimum core obligation to ensure the satisfaction of, at the very least, minimum essential levels of each of the rights is incumbent upon every State party. Thus, for example, a State party in which any significant number of individuals is deprived of essential foodstuffs, of essential primary health care, of

---

[35] *Soobramoney v Minister of Health (Kwazulu-Natal)* [1997] ZACC 17 at para 8.

basic shelter and housing, or of the most basic forms of education is, prima facie, failing to discharge its obligations under the Covenant. If the Covenant were to be read in such a way as not to establish such a minimum core obligation, it would be largely deprived of its raison d'être'.[36] This doctrine thus establishes enforceable obligations on states that relate to a minimum threshold of provision that all can claim relatively quickly to ensure the needs of the greatest urgency are provided for whilst allowing the full realisation of the rights to be achieved over time.

That approach has been followed, for instance, in Colombia in the *T-025 of 2004* case. The case dealt with the claims by a large number of people who were internally displaced due to ongoing armed conflict in the country. These people claimed that their socio-economic rights in the Constitution were not being realised. The Colombian Constitutional Court articulated a general standard that must be met in relation to socio-economic rights but also realised that it will not be possible immediately to give effect to that standard. It, therefore recognised that some prioritisation would be necessary in relation to the social economic rights of internally displaced people in Colombia. The court also realised that, whilst it could set the parameters for the realisation of these rights, it needed to harness the capacities of other branches of government in setting the concrete standards required to give effect to these rights. It thus sought to balance the need to provide guidance to other branches about the expectations of what they are required to do whilst providing space for them to fulfil their functions.

The court thus recognised that 'it will not always be possible to satisfy, in a simultaneous manner and to the maximum possible level, the positive obligations imposed by all the constitutional rights of the entire displaced population, given the material restrictions at hand…'.[37] Nevertheless, a minimum level of the rights of the IDPs had to be protected immediately. These minimum levels 'are those that have a close connection with the preservation of life under elementary conditions of dignity as distinct and autonomous human beings'.[38] The court held importantly that '[i]t is there, in the preservation of the most basic conditions that permit a dignified survival, where a clear limit must be drawn between the State obligations towards the displaced population of imperative and urgent compliance, and those which, even though they must be fulfilled, do not have the same priority…'. This reasoning was then used to identify a number of minimum rights – including the right to life, a basic level of subsistence, essential medical services and sanitation – that had to be realised as a matter of urgency through positive action on the part of the state.

In the face of a lack of government capacity even to determine what was required as well as a lack of resources, the Constitutional Court of Colombia

[36] General Comment No 3 on the Nature of States Parties' Obligations Under Article 2, Paragraph 1 of the ICESCR by the UN Economic and Social Council at para 10 (available at: https://www.refworld.org/legal/general/cescr/1990/en/5613accessed at 07.04.2025).

[37] Decision *T-025 of 2004* (note 8 above) at section 9.

[38] Ibid.

recognised that it was its role to give greater determinacy to the obligations imposed by socio-economic rights and greater guidance to the government as to what it was obliged to do. It also made a number of findings of unconstitutionality in the government's conduct, providing it with an understanding of what it needed to do to rectify its behaviour. It, nevertheless, still allowed some flexibility to the government as to how to concretise the broad standards that it set. Importantly, in the Global South, given the significant limitations of resources, the approach adopted by the ICESCR and Colombian Constitutional Court evidences the need for a two-tier approach to be adopted towards providing content to rights: the first tier deals with those needs and interests which have the greatest priority and must be fulfilled in the shorter term; the second tier articulates those needs and interests which remain vitally important but which can be realised in the medium term. The provision of the first tier to individuals enables their being placed in a position where their most urgent interests are taken care of and so, allows, some time for the fulfilment of the second tier.

2. Limited Content and A Flexible Review Standard: South Africa

Another response to the difficult circumstances in the Global South is for courts to avoid providing any detailed content to socio-economic rights. Such an approach preserves maximum flexibility for other branches – and the courts – to respond to the dual problems of lack of capacity and resources. This approach does not seek to articulate any firm entitlements that individuals have: instead, it sees socio-economic rights as granting courts a broad discretion to review government decision-making and intervene where it deems necessary. It also places less emphasis on explicating legal doctrine and more emphasis on developing remedies that work. It also can require greater participation in decision-making to address some of the problems involved.

There is an obvious problem with this approach in that it is not clear when to grant remedies if the entitlements themselves are not clear. Courts, in these circumstances, do not articulate a clear understanding of these rights and prefer an ad hoc method of addressing problems as they arise. Over time, these ad hoc decision-making and remedies disclose some conception of what these rights are designed to guarantee. The advantages of this approach relate to flexibility, responding to particular crises and gradual development of content. The disadvantages of this approach are also manifest: It is not clear what the basis will be for particular decisions being made which, in turn, will mean that the ability to guide other branches of government and courts in future cases, will be very limited – at least in the initial stages of such an approach being utilized.

This approach has in fact been adopted by the South African Constitutional Court. Its famous *Grootboom* decision related to a challenge to the government's existing programme to deliver housing for failing to cater to individuals who are homeless and in desperate circumstances. The Court focused on two aspects of the obligations of the government in this regard. First, it held that the government has a duty to develop a programme in relation to each particular socio-economic right: Such a programme requires a government to develop a coherent policy approach to realising these rights.[39] That fits into the conception of judicial review I have articulated through essentially requiring other branches to perform their tasks.

The Court then secondly stated that it will only review such a programme on the basis of whether it was reasonable or not and it provided some criteria for determining the reasonableness of a program.[40] Those criteria overlap to some extent with what was articulated in the *Hartz IV* decision: requiring clear and justifiable means for achieving the goal sought to be achieved. They also involve a degree of equality in that no major group must be excluded from a policy; and a degree of priority to those whose needs are most urgent. The court has, however, refused to articulate detailed content in relation to socio-economic rights and the reasonableness standard, whilst embracing a range of different factors, is a broad overarching review standard that creates significant discretion for judges when applying it. It has led to decisions which come close to articulating a strong right that individuals have to have their desperate needs prioritised – such as in *Grootboom* – to decisions where the standard seems to require very little of the government – such as in the recent case of *Thubakgale*.[41] The Court's approach seems designed to maximise the policy space open to government whilst preserving an opportunity for the court to intervene in circumstances where there has been a significant failure to exercise governmental authority properly. The Court recognises problems in the capacity surrounding decision-making of the government through this doctrine and preserves the space for its own interventions. Nevertheless, at the same time, it, in some sense, strengthens the difficulty facing other branches by failing to set standards where they are lacking or to prioritise more urgent needs where they have been ignored. The ad hoc flexible nature of the approach thus fails to provide guidance where it is clearly needed in a civil service that lacks significant skills. In the face of widespread incapacity, its approach also potentially entrenches failures of decision-making by placing emphasis continually on deference to the decision-maker and, intervening, only on infrequent occasions.

Thus, the circumstances prevalent in the Global South – of high levels of resource scarcity as well as incapacity – can lead to divergent responses in relation to the determining of the content of rights by judges. The one approach is to determine more concrete standards and priorities and to provide stronger definitions of the content of the right. The second approach is to refuse to engage in standard-setting and prioritisation and to focus on flaws in government decision-making. The second approach has a clear problem in not being able to articulate

---

[39] *Grootboom* (note 9 above) at paras 39–42.

[40] *Grootboom* (note 9 above) at paras 43–46, 54–56 and 63–66.

[41] *Thubakgale v Ekurhuleni Metropolitan Municipality* [2021] ZACC 45 ('*Thubakgale*').

standards against which to identify such flaws in government decision-making. It also fails to provide an understanding of what individuals can claim from these rights. It also produces insufficiently justified decision. In order to have an effect, however, it is often coupled with a stronger approach towards remedies, the matter to which I now turn.

3. Remedies for Socio-Economic Rights in the Global South

In the face of the twin difficulties of resources and capacity, courts in the Global South often spend less time on articulating legal principles and doctrine and focus on remedies that address the problems blocking the realisation of rights. We will first consider the problem that resources and capacity causes for remedies and then some of the approaches that have been adopted.

a) Resource Shortages and Remedies

The problem of the lack of resources places courts in great difficulty when seeking to give an efficient and effective remedy. In the rare cases where there is absolute scarcity, there are simply no resources available to give effect to the court order. Most cases however are not ones of absolute scarcity – where the state has no resources at its disposal – but ones where the level of scarcity involved requires re-allocation of resources from one sphere to another. Reallocation is easier where it is clear that there are resources being devoted to areas which are not of a high priority: for instance, buying expensive cars for politicians and ministers. It is much more difficult when it comes to reallocating resources between expenditure which all can be of great importance: housing, healthcare, education, the justice system, and the police are amongst the legitimate areas where the government needs to expend resources. Courts cannot ultimately determine the fine-grained allocations of budget within the state. They can, however, provide some guidance on particularly urgent areas that socio-economic rights require be prioritised. This approach relates to the question of determining priorities and one type of remedy is for courts to declare that existing government programmes fail adequately to prioritise in the way that they are required to. In circumstances where there is not absolute scarcity, such an approach can help address the worst forms of vulnerability such as homelessness, hunger and thirst. In such circumstances and where urgent need exists, courts may well give more intrusive orders that place specific requirements on the government – as was done by the Colombian Constitutional Court in *T-025 of 2004*. Even then, in relation to budgeting, some degree of leeway and discretion was granted to the government in determining how to allocate resources in this regard.

b) The Problem of Capacity and Remedies

The problem of capacity also creates a range of conundrums. Drawing on the work of Chris Hansen, Roach and Budlender have helpfully broken the problem down into three dimensions where government officials are inattentive, where they are incompetent, and where they are intransigent.[42] They suggest that courts can respond to these problems with different forms of remedy. This analysis is compelling but I want to focus a little bit more on the incompetence issue which goes to the heart of the capacity question. Many Global South countries simply lack the skills in the civil service adequately to deliver on the mandates of the government. The skills shortage often comes from a historical legacy relating to a lack of education, flight of skills internationally as well as a flight of skills from the public sector to the private sector. Institutional cultures of a lack of transparency and accountability often contribute to this malaise – where officials, are employed, for a specific purpose, they fail adequately to perform their jobs without any consequences. These problems often permeate throughout the executive and become entrenched, rendering it very difficult for the executive alone to address them. Whilst the executive is technically accountable to the legislature, legislative processes are often ill-suited to address a malaise in delivery by the executive. There is also an institutional problem in that, in many political systems, the executive political leadership is often elected by the majority of Parliament and so there is a less of an incentive to highlight areas of malperformance. It thus seems evident that another external body must step in to address this malaise.

In some countries, as has been mentioned, there has been the creation of fourth branch institutions such as an ombudsperson which have powers to investigate and make orders in relation to executive failures. These institutions usually operate at the level of an individual case and sometimes are quite effective in addressing problems faced by individuals. They, however struggle to address some of the systemic issues plaguing the executive. Problems of systemic incapacity often reach the courts and the question is what to courts can do. The Colombian Court has adopted a doctrine for these circumstances, recognising that a particular systemic malaise may be evidence of an unconstitutional state of affairs. Once declared, however, there is a question as to what courts can do to remedy the problem it has identified. It is important first to recognise the problem in order to understand that the role of courts must be different in countries facing these problems. The question then is what courts can do to respond.

aa) Diagnosing the Root Cause

Systemic incapacity may require trying to understand the root of the problem. The Constitutional Court of South Africa's case of *Nokotyana* dealt with one such instance:[43] A community applied to court for an order providing sufficient temporary toilets in the community and lighting to deter crime. The central problem lay in the fact that the provincial government had not made a determi-

[42] *Roach and Budlender* (note 32 above) at 345–351.

[43] *Nokotyana v Ekurhuleni Metropolitan Municipality* [2009] ZACC 33.

nation about the upgrading of the informal settlement in which they lived, which would have addressed the complaints of the community. Instead of ordering the government to provide the toilets and lighting, the court ordered the provincial government to make a decision on the upgrading of the settlement. This order thus sought to go to the source of the reason for the lack of delivery.

The difficulty with the order is that it failed to grapple at all with the reasons for the failure to make a decision by the government: what was blocking the executive decision-making and why had a decision not been taken for many years? The court simply ordered a decision to be taken without engaging with the reasons the decision had not been taken. Such an approach may well be entirely ineffective as the administration is not capable of doing what the court asks it to do. Even if it does so, it cannot adequately implement the decision. Consequently, the Court's approach did not go far enough: it recognised the central blockage but did not seek to understand what was underlying the failure to take a decision. It also failed adequately to address the plight of people in the interim pending the decision – addressing the root cause of a problem should not obscure the urgent needs of individuals that require attention pending a full resolution of their plight.

bb) Participation in Decision-making

Another possible approach to incapacity is to widen the actors involved and encourage greater participation in decision-making. The South African Constitutional Court has interpreted its 'reasonableness' standard to require participation by vulnerable individuals in decisions that affect them and to force the government to engage with individuals in arriving at solutions that impact their socio-economic rights. This approach has been utilized where individuals have been threatened with eviction: in South Africa, courts require there to be meaningful engagement between the individuals concerned and the government to arrive at a solution that ensures individuals are not rendered homeless.[44] The benefit of such a remedy is that it seeks to address the exclusion of vulnerable and poor people from decision-making surrounding their lives and a heavy-handed approach by the government. Instead of imposing specific solutions on parties, it enables them to determine, through negotiation, the optimal resolution to their disputes. Participation can be seen to empower individuals to become involved in making decisions about their own lives.[45] It can also enable individuals to be involved in making decisions about priorities in their lives – thus addressing the problem of resources – as well as placing officials in direct relation with individ-

---

[44] *Port Elizabeth Municipality v Various Occupiers* [2004] ZACC 7; *Occupiers of 51 Olivia Road, Berea Township and 197 Main Street Johannesburg v City of Johannesburg* [2008] ZACC 1.

[45] *Ray* 'Evictions, Aspirations and Avoidance' (2013) 5 Constitutional Court Review 173 at 204.

uals whose lives they affect through their decisions. That direct engagement can place some degree of accountability on the officials. Whilst not a full solution to the problem of capacity, it potentially allows individuals to identify problems in this regard and engage with officials as to how to solve them.

cc) Supervision

In the face of widespread incapacity, it is tempting for courts to intervene directly to solve the problem. As we saw, the problem partially arises from a lack of accountability and oversight over performance due to failures in the executive's hierarchy and performance management. To address this issue, courts may supervise the implementation of their orders though not take over the function themselves. In the Colombian case of *T-025 of 2004*, the Constitutional Court of Colombia provided detailed guidance as to what was required by the government and has retained supervision over the implementation of its order ever since it was given in 2004. This approach has been seen to provide widespread improvements in government co-ordination and budgeting and to have had a large impact.[46]

The South African Constitutional Court was also faced with a serious breakdown in the system of providing social grants to individuals. The minister in question who was responsible was herself part of the problem and in fact a personal costs order was awarded against her for her dereliction of duty.[47] Given the widespread impact that the breakdown of such a system could cause, the Court required continual reporting from the ministry to ensure that the system was able to deliver those grants to the beneficiaries. That supervision had the benefit of encouraging transparency as well as placing external oversight over a dysfunctional department. The Constitutional Court, in this case, also assumed control over determining that a private company which had been contracted to provide the grants did not abuse its position and make untoward profit from what was a flawed procurement process.[48]

These supervisory orders can to some extent address incapacity problems by placing a spotlight upon them and monitoring performance. They, of course, cannot make up for a shortfall in skills and the ability of individuals to deliver. Such orders also place major burdens on judges continually to supervise the implementation of their orders and, in some sense, to assume the function of

---

[46] *Rodriguez-Garavito* 'Beyond the Courtroom: the Impact of Judicial Activism on Socio-Economic Rights in Latin America' (2011) 89 Texas Law Review 1669 at 1682–1688. For a less positive assessment, see *Beltrán* 'Forced Displacement and Social Change: Light and Shadows in the Implementation of the Judgment *T-025 of 2004*' in Bilchitz and Cachalia Transitional Justice, Distributive Justice and Transformative Constitutionalism: Comparing Colombia and South Africa (Oxford University Press, 2023) 276 at 294–295.

[47] *Black Sash Trust v Minister of Social Development (Freedom Under Law Intervening)* [2018] ZACC 36.

[48] *AllPay Consolidated Investment Holdings (Pty) Ltd v Chief Executive Officer of the South African Social Security Agency (No 2)* [2014] ZACC 12 at para 78.

other branches of government together with their already consuming obligations. For this reason, in systems with widespread incapacity, supervision cannot be adopted over all government departments.

dd) Appointing Skilled Personnel to Manage Executive Performance

To address the above-mentioned problems, at times, the courts in the Global South have, in fact, appointed people with a high level of skills to monitor the implementation of programmes to deliver socio-economic rights.[49] One of the most notable instances in this regard is the famous right to food case in India. In the face of widespread destruction of grain that could not be exported, the Supreme Court of India made a number of far-reaching orders that sought to guarantee every individual in India the right to food.[50] These orders included the provision of midday meals at school for children as well as a guarantee of a minimum level of food or income to individuals in the society. Due to widespread government incapacity and inefficiency, the Supreme Court appointed specific commissioners who were responsible for overseeing the implementation of their orders. These commissioners were experts in the area and could complement government capacity in this regard. This order is an example of where courts actually appoint people to take over the implementation of a programme and so address directly the problem of incapacity. In South Africa, in response to widespread dysfunction in relation to land reform, the Constitutional Court issued a similar order where it appointed what it termed a special master to oversee the implementation of its orders in this area.[51]

Orders appointing skilled personnel could help relieve the pressure on courts – which are busy with their day-to-day hearings and decisions – from having to take on the task that should be assigned to other branches of government. They, to an extent, though require courts to identify persons with the relevant skills which can itself be a problem. Such orders can also elicit some conflict where there is a refusal by the department to work properly together with the appointed official.

c) Corruption and Socio-Economic Rights

It is important to recognise that in many Global South countries it is not just a lack of skills that is the issue. There is a diversion of resources through corruption from the public sector to the private sector and to corrupt politicians. The adequate enforcement of socio-economic rights requires addressing this problem as

[49] *Maphosa* 'Are Judicial Monitoring Institutions A Legitimate Remedy For Addressing Systemic Socioeconomic Rights Violations?' (2021) 4 South African Journal on Human Rights 362 at 363.

[50] *People's Union for Civil Liberties v Union of India* (2004) 12 *SC India* 108.

[51] *Mwelase v Director-General for the Department of Rural Development and Land Reform* [2019] ZACC 30.

limited resources are diverted from the delivery of goods and services to corrupt individuals and government authority is misused.[52] Indeed, in the Global South, judicial accountability surrounding procurement processes and criminal law enforcement around corruption can be essential necessary conditions for the effective enforcement of socio-economic rights. The holding of high officials of state to account can be an important prong in insisting on the realisation of socio-economic rights: in South Africa, the recognition that the president had utilized public resources for private purposes can be understood partially as a decision to ensure the effective use of public resources for the purposes for which they are intended.[53]

D. Comparing the Global North and Global South: Perils for Scholarship

This paper began by asserting the universality of socio-economic rights. Everyone, no matter where they live, is entitled to the resources necessary to live a life of dignity and to flourish. That is a principle which all societies around the world should affirm. Where socio-economic rights are included within constitutions, judges are under a duty to give effect to this principle.

At the same time, I argue that there are two central differences between Global North and Global South societies of relevance in this context: first, a significant disparity in resources; and, secondly, a significant difference in government capacity. These differences affect the level of realisation of socio-economic rights that can be achieved in each society as well as the manner in which that can be done. When considering the enforcement of these rights by judges, it is necessary to consider these central differences. I have argued that these differences shift the task to be performed by judges: in the Global North, their task is similar to that in relation to other rights and largely involves the protection of vulnerable/minority groups and individuals from insufficient attention by the majoritarian structures. In the Global South, however, the task is much more expansive and focused on the effective realisation of these rights: it requires often addressing the exclusion of majorities from adequate protection through democratic structures; building and enabling these structures to function and, at times, intervening in the very dysfunction of these structures. These differences in task affect how they address the twin difficulties of developing the content of these rights as well as the remedies they grant to give effect to these rights. As we saw, given the expansive task and recent engagement with them, there have been divergent approaches amongst countries in the Global South. In relation to content, some seek to

[52] *Glenister v President of the Republic of South Africa* [2011] ZACC 6.

[53] *Economic Freedom Fighters v Speaker of the National Assembly, Democratic Alliance v Speaker of the National Assembly* [2016] ZACC 11.

provide more guidance on what is required to other branches and engage in the question of prioritisation; others focus on preserving maximum flexibility to intervene when decision-making is flawed. In relation to remedy, we saw that the lack of resources creates problems for strong remedies; whilst the lack of capacity encourages greater intervention in addressing the inability to deliver. The contrast in approaches suggests that the Global South is not uniform in responding to the common challenges facing these societies. The Global North/Global South distinction thus does not track a neat delineation between different approaches. At the same time, the lack of uniformity is useful in comparing which approaches are more successful or not in addressing the problems facing these societies.

It is interesting to consider what can be learnt from comparing the Global South and the Global North and the perils of too simplistic comparisons in this regard. It is at the outset important to recognise one of the enduring legacies of colonialism and that is epistemic power imbalances. As Bonilla has outlined, Global South societies are often understood to be drawing on the theory in the Global North and simply applying it.[54] Moreover, greater value is granted to knowledge produced in the Global North over that in the Global South.[55] Given the differences in task and context, it is hard to see how the theory behind socio-economic rights can simply be applied from the Global North to the Global South. Moreover, the value of knowledge produced in the Global North becomes questionable. Nevertheless, one should not ignore these dynamics nor the effects they have on courts and the jurisprudence that results.

Given the underdevelopment of socio-economic rights in the Global North, there has been limited influence of theory and doctrine in this regard. Nevertheless, one should not underestimate the influence of a Northern conception of the separation of powers on the Global South courts. A simplistic approach to the separation of powers drawn from the North can be seen to underpin, for instance, the failure of the Constitutional Court of South Africa to develop more detailed content to socio-economic rights, finding that it is inappropriate to do so.[56] That simplistic approach, has in a society that direly needs the strong enforcement of these rights, come close to denuding them of meaning.[57] I have sought to highlight in this article how the approach to the separation of powers and the judicial role has to be sensitive to the particular challenges facing the society and a once-size-fits-all approach cannot work. Academic scholarship, given the power dynamics

---

[54] He terms this the assumption of the 'production well': see *Maldonado* 'Toward a Constitutionalism of the Global South' in Maldonado Constitutionalism of the Global South: The Activist Tribunals of India, South Africa, and Colombia (Cambridge University Press, 2013) 1 at 12.

[55] He refers to this as the assumption of 'protected geographical indication': ibid. at 12–13.

[56] *Mazibuko v City of Johannesburg* [2009] ZACC 28. See, in this regard, *Williams* 'The Role of Courts in the Quantitative Implementation of Social and Economic Rights: a Comparative Study' (2010) 3 Constitutional Court Review 141 at 189.

[57] *Thubakgale* (note 41 above).

at issue, has also often prioritised the concerns of the North – around their conception of the separation of powers, legitimacy and competence – over the concerns of the South – the effective alleviation of poverty. That has led, for instance, to a division between Global South and Global North scholars in their response to the South African case law with the former lauding it and the latter being much more critical.[58]

There is a lot of potential for the Global South to influence the Global North in relation to these rights. As is evident, there has been an experimentation with different approaches which provide a rich tapestry for Global North courts to draw on. To the extent that conditions in some Northern countries have similarities to the South, these are useful experiences. At the same time, there is a need to recognise the differences in situatedness and the impact that has on the task of courts. Courts in the Global North can afford to be more ambitious in realising these rights and do not have to address the problems of incapacity facing courts in the South. At the same time, there may be less justification for as intrusive interventions with decision-making by the legislature and executive given they do not suffer from the same level of dysfunction.

I have assumed a perspective in which states are separate from one another – there are of course obligations on Global North states to assist Global South states to realise these rights. Perhaps Global North courts can adopt a more stringent approach in this regard particularly in light of retrogressive steps such as the recent reductions in the foreign aid budgets of Global North countries. Moreover, Global North states can help address some of the capacity problems faced by Global South states. It can perhaps be hoped that over time there is a greater convergence in the tasks to be achieved in giving effect to socio-economic rights and their realisation. Until that time arrives, scholars, judges and other decision-makers must be mindful of these different realities in order to adequately give effect to socio-economic rights in their societies.

---

[58] See *Landau* 'South African Social Rights and the Global Canon: A Revisionist View' in Dixon and Roux Constitutional Triumphs, Constitutional Disappointments: A Critical Assessment of the 1996 South African Constitution's Local and International Influence (Cambridge University Press, 2018) 406 at 415–416. Some scholars have, unfortunately, almost exclusively referenced scholars in the Global North, for instance, when engaging with the South African socio-economic rights Jurisprudence: see *Moyn* Not Enough: Human Rights in an Unequal World (Oxford University Press, 2018) 200 (fn 32).

List of Contributors

Philipp Dann, Professor Dr., LL.M., Humboldt-Universität zu Berlin, Germany
Konrad Lachmayer Professor. Dr., Sigmund Freud Privatuniversität Wien, Austria
Pablo Riberi, Professor Dr., LL.M., National University of Córdoba, Argentina
Surya Deva, Professor, Ph.D., Macquarie Law School, UN Special Rapporteur on the Right to Development, Sydney, Australia
Selin Esen, Professor Dr., Ankara University, Turkey
David Bilchitz, Professor, Ph.D., University of Johannesburg, South Africa